Deep Sleep

Other Titles from SWEET Institute Publishing

- Always Enough: The Transformational Power of Unconditional Positive Regard
- Before Anything Else, Validate: The Missing Link in Healing, Leadership, Relationships, and Personal Growth
- Discovering Your Worth: Everything You Need to Feel Fulfilled
- Emotional Intelligence: The Inner Science of Transformation
- Journey to Empowerment
- Life Is Not Hard: A New Blueprint for Living with Ease, Meaning, and Freedom
- One Habit at a Time: The Art and Science of Sustainable Change
- Remembering: The Journey Back to the Pre-Conditioned Self
- The Secret Is in Remembering: Why We Suffer, Why We Forget, and How to Return to Who We Are
- Worthy: From Self-Doubt to Self-Respect
- Beyond Burnout: The Inside-Out Revolution in Work, Healing, and Meaning
- The Joy We Bring: Rediscovering the Power of Joy in Everyday Life

SWEET Institute Publishing
Transformational Books for a Transformational World

Deep Sleep

How to Calm the Nervous System, Quiet the Mind, and Restore Rest Through the Four Layers of Transformation

By

Mardoche Sidor, MD
Karen Dubin, PhD, LCSW
The SWEET Institute

SWEET Institute Publishing
Transformational Books for a Transformational World

Published by:

SWEET Institute Publishing
New York, NY
www.SWEETInstitutePublishing.com

First Edition
Printed in the United States of America

ISBN (Paperback): 978-1-968105-36-5
ISBN (Hardcover): 978-1-968105-37-2
ISBN (eBook): 978-1-968105-38-9

Library of Congress Control Number: 2026946080

Cover Design by SWEET Institute Publishing
Interior Design and Layout by SWEET Institute Publishing

For bulk orders, permissions, or media inquiries, please contact:

sweetinstitutepublishing@sweetinstitute.com

Unless otherwise noted, all stories and case examples in this book are either fictionalized or used with permission. Identifying details have been changed to protect the privacy of individuals.

SWEET Institute Publishing
Transformational Books for a Transformational World

SWEET Institute Publishing — Universal Disclaimer

Dedication

To everyone who has ever stared at the ceiling in the middle of the night, wondering why sleep would not come.

To those whose minds would not quiet, whose hearts carried too much, whose bodies remained on guard long after the danger had passed.

To those who felt exhausted but could not rest, tired but unable to sleep, busy but disconnected, successful but depleted.

This book is for you.

It is also dedicated to the countless clinicians, caregivers, teachers, parents, healers, and helpers who spend their days caring for others while often forgetting to care for themselves.

And to every person who has ever felt trapped in survival mode, may you discover that your nervous system is not broken. It has been trying to protect you all along.

May these pages help you remember what your body has always known - rest is not weakness, stillness is not danger, peace is possible, and you do not have to earn the right to sleep.

Most of all, may you come to know that deep sleep is more than a biological necessity. It is a return to safety, to wholeness, and a return to yourself.

With gratitude,

Mardoche Sidor, MD
Karen Dubin, Ph.D., LCSW
The SWEET Institute

Deep Sleep

We do not lose sleep because the body forgets how.
We lose sleep because the body remembers.
It remembers the stress.
the pressure,
the unfinished conversations,
the fears we pushed aside,
the grief we never fully felt,
the beliefs we never questioned,
the life we have been trying to carry alone.

Sleep is not merely a biological process.
It is a relationship,
A relationship with the body,
A relationship with the mind,
a relationship with our history,
a relationship with meaning.

And when these relationships begin to heal,
the nervous system finally discovers what it has been seeking all along: Safety.

For deep sleep is not what happens when we force the body to rest.
Deep sleep is what happens when the body no longer believes it must remain awake.

The goal is not to force sleep.
The goal is to become safe enough to receive it.

Mardoche Sidor, MD
Karen Dubin, Ph.D., LCSW
The SWEET Institute

Table of Contents

Preface

By Mardoche Sidor, MD

For much of my professional life, I have been fascinated by a question that at first seems deceptively simple: Why can't people sleep?

As a psychiatrist, I have sat with thousands of individuals over the course of nearly twenty years. Some struggled with depression, and others struggled with anxiety, trauma, addiction, grief, relationship difficulties, burnout, loneliness, chronic medical conditions, or the countless challenges that accompany being human.

Yet regardless of the diagnosis, one complaint appeared again and again, "I can't sleep."

Some could not fall asleep. Some could not stay asleep. Some woke up at three in the morning and could not return to sleep. Others slept through the night but woke feeling exhausted, as though they had spent the entire night fighting an invisible battle.

At first, I approached sleep the way many clinicians are trained to approach it. I learned about sleep hygiene, circadian rhythms, neurotransmitters, sleep disorders, medications, cognitive behavioral therapy for insomnia, relaxation techniques, and the growing science of sleep medicine.

All of these approaches matter. Many of them work. Many of them help tremendously. However, over time, I began noticing something else. Sleep problems were rarely just sleep problems.

A person struggling with sleep was often struggling with life. The executive who could not shut off his mind at night was carrying enormous pressure and responsibility. The woman waking every night at 2:00 a.m. often carried years of unresolved grief. The man who could not relax enough to fall asleep had spent much of his life preparing for danger. The exhausted caregiver had forgotten how to care for herself. The high achiever who seemed successful in every area of life often carried an internal dialogue so relentless that even sleep could not provide relief. Again and again, I discovered that sleep was not merely biological. It was psychological, relational, environmental, and existential.

Sleep was often the place where everything else showed up. The body was speaking. The nervous system was communicating. And many people had never learned how to listen.

This realization changed how I thought about sleep. It also changed how I thought about healing.

As the years passed, my work expanded beyond psychiatry into education, psychotherapy, leadership development, organizational transformation, and the work of the SWEET Institute.

Across all of these settings, I observed the same pattern.

People were exhausted, and not only physically, but emotionally exhausted, mentally exhausted, spiritually exhausted, relationally exhausted, and existentially exhausted.

Many were functioning. Many were succeeding. Many were accomplishing remarkable things. Yet underneath the surface, countless people were living in a state of chronic activation. Their nervous systems had forgotten how to rest. Some had been living this way for years. Others for decades. And many had begun believing that this was simply normal.

I did not write this book because I believe sleep is important. I wrote this book because I believe sleep reveals something profound about how we are living.

When we cannot sleep, it is often because some part of us remains awake: a worried mind, a vigilant nervous system, an unresolved grief, an unprocessed fear, a conditioned belief, an overloaded life, a neglected need, and a forgotten self.

The deeper I explored sleep, the more convinced I became that healing requires a broader framework than most people have been offered. At the SWEET Institute, we use what we call the Four Layers of Transformation.

The conscious layer focuses on behaviors, routines, habits, lifestyle changes, and daily practices.

The pre-conscious layer explores the schemas, beliefs, emotional patterns, attachment styles, and psychological conditioning that quietly shape experience.

The unconscious layer examines the deeper emotional material that often lives outside awareness: our defenses, unresolved conflicts, dreams, emotional wounds, and hidden fears.

Finally, the existential layer invites us to examine meaning, purpose, freedom, responsibility, values, and the deeper questions of human existence.

Through years of teaching, clinical work, and personal reflection, I became convinced that lasting change occurs when all four layers are addressed.

Sleep is no exception. Many books will teach you how to improve your sleep. This book will do that. But my hope is that it will also help you understand why your sleep may have become disrupted in the first place. My hope is that it will help you develop a healthier relationship with your body, your mind, your emotions, your history, and your life. My hope is that it will help you stop fighting yourself, for one of the greatest lessons I have learned as a psychiatrist is that healing rarely occurs through force. It occurs through understanding, through awareness, through compassion, through practice, and through integration.

Most importantly, I hope this book helps you remember something that many exhausted people have forgotten: Your nervous system is not your enemy. Your body is not betraying you. Your symptoms are not evidence of weakness. More often than not, they are evidence of adaptation.

They are the result of a nervous system that has worked tirelessly to protect you, and perhaps too tirelessly. The good news is that nervous systems can learn. Brains can change. Patterns can soften. Sleep can return. Hope can return. Peace can return. And sometimes, what begins as a search for better sleep becomes something much larger: A journey back to yourself.

Thank you for allowing us to accompany you on that journey. May these pages help you sleep more deeply. May they help you live more fully; and may they remind you that rest is not something you must earn. Rather, it is something you were always meant to experience.

Mardoche Sidor, MD
Quadruple Board-Certified Psychiatrist,
Former Assistant Clinical Professor of Psychiatry at Columbia University, Vagelos College of Physicians and Surgeons,
Current Psychoanalytic Candidate at Columbia University
Founder of the SWEET Institute
Chief Medical Officer at Urban Pathways

The Four Layers of Transformation Pyramid

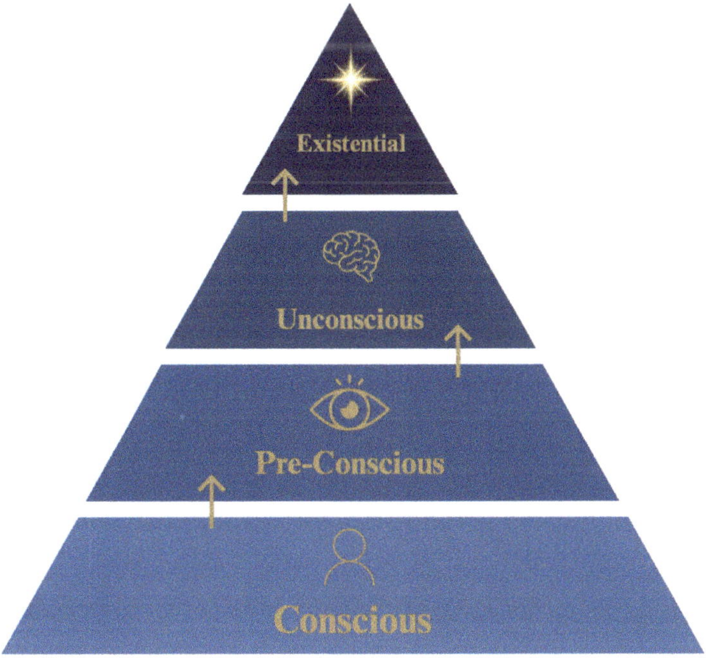

Lasting change occurs when all four layers are addressed

Introduction

Imagine for a moment that tonight, when your head touches the pillow, your body softens naturally. Your breathing slows, your mind quiets, and your nervous system releases the day.

You drift into sleep, not because you forced it, not because you exhausted yourself, not because you escaped into distraction, but because your body finally feels safe enough to rest.

For many people, that image feels almost impossible. Millions of individuals struggle every night with falling asleep, staying asleep, waking too early, restless sleep, nightmares, racing thoughts, nighttime anxiety, emotional activation, or waking up exhausted despite spending enough hours in bed. Many have tried everything: sleep hygiene, melatonin, meditation apps, and white noise. Many have tried herbal remedies, special pillows, special mattresses, and sleep trackers. Many have also tried supplements, and medications; and some have experienced relief, while others continue searching.

If you are reading this book, chances are you have spent at least some time searching too. We want you to know something immediately: You are not broken. Your body is not failing you. Your nervous system is not your enemy.

In fact, one of the central ideas of this book is that your sleep difficulties may be making perfect sense. It may not be pleasant or desirable, but it is understandable, for sleep problems rarely exist in isolation.

Sleep is influenced by everything: your biology, your thoughts, your emotions, and your relationships. It is also influenced by your environment, your habits, and your history. It is influenced by your beliefs, your purpose, your relationship with uncertainty, and your relationship with yourself.

In other words, sleep is where life shows up, and that is what makes this book different. Most books on sleep focus primarily on what happens at the conscious level. They teach routines, habits, behaviors, schedules, nutrition, exercise, light exposure, sleep hygiene, and practical strategies. These are important. We discuss all of them. However, at the SWEET Institute, we have learned that lasting transformation requires going deeper.

Human beings are layered, and healing is layered. That understanding gave rise to what we call the Four Layers of Transformation.

The first layer is the Conscious Layer. This is the layer of behaviors, routines, habits, goals, decisions, accountability, structure, discipline, and lifestyle changes. This is where most sleep interventions begin.

The second layer is the Pre-Conscious Layer. This is the layer of emotional patterns, attachment styles, core beliefs, schemas, conditioned expectations, and internal narratives. Many people cannot sleep because their minds and nervous systems have learned patterns that keep them activated.

The third layer is the Unconscious Layer. This is the layer of unresolved emotional experiences, repressed feelings, defenses, dreams, hidden fears, and the psychological material that often lives outside awareness but continues influencing behavior and physiology. Sometimes the body stays awake because some part of the self remains unheard.

The fourth layer is the Existential Layer. This is the layer of meaning, purpose, freedom, responsibility, identity, values, and the deeper questions of human existence. Many people are not merely tired. They are exhausted by lives that have become disconnected from meaning.

True healing often requires addressing all four layers. This framework guides the entire book. However, it is not the only framework you will encounter. Throughout these pages, we will also use the SWEET Multi-Domain Model, which recognizes that every human experience occurs simultaneously across five interconnected domains, Biological, Psychological, Relational, Environmental, and Existential.

When sleep improves in one domain, it often improves in the others. When one domain remains neglected, healing may stall.

You will also encounter the SWEET Body–Mind–Meaning Framework, which serves as the organizing language of this book. The body must feel regulated. The mind must become more flexible. Meaning must become more coherent. When these three dimensions align, profound healing becomes possible.

Finally, we will repeatedly return to the SWEET SDAF Framework: Stabilize → Decide → Act → Feel. Many people try to make decisions while dysregulated. They try to change behavior while overwhelmed. They try to think clearly while emotionally flooded.

The SDAF framework teaches a different sequence. First stabilize. Then decide. Then act. Then experience the emotional consequences of aligned action. This simple sequence can transform sleep and many other aspects of life.

As you move through this book, you will notice that it is not written like a traditional textbook. It is also not written like a traditional self-help book.

Instead, it combines science, stories, conversations, reflections, practical exercises, clinical wisdom, neuroscience, psychology, and lived human experience.

You will encounter the research. You will encounter practical tools, and you will encounter questions that may challenge you. Most importantly, you will encounter opportunities to move beyond intellectual understanding and into lived experience, for knowledge alone rarely changes lives; rather, implementation changes lives, experience changes lives, and practice changes lives.

Transformation occurs when insight becomes embodied, and that is why every chapter includes opportunities for reflection, awareness, and action. We encourage you not to rush through this book. Read slowly. Pause often. Reflect honestly. Experiment consistently; and notice what resonates. Notice what challenges you, and notice what your nervous system is trying to teach you.

This book is not simply about sleep. It is about restoration, regulation, and healing. It is about reclaiming a relationship with your body. It is about learning how to listen to your nervous system rather than fight it.

It is about creating a life that supports rest rather than constantly demanding recovery; and perhaps most importantly, it is about remembering that rest is not something you must earn. Rest is part of your birthright.

Whether you are a clinician, a caregiver, a parent, a leader, a student, a person living with insomnia, or simply someone longing to wake up feeling restored again, we wrote this book for you. We invite you to approach these pages with curiosity, with patience, with compassion, and with hope.

No matter how long you have struggled, healing remains possible. The nervous system can learn. The body can change. Sleep can return. And sometimes, what begins as a search for better sleep becomes the beginning of a much larger journey: a journey back to safety, a journey back to wholeness, and a journey back to yourself.

Welcome. Let us begin.

Before You Turn This Page

This book can be read in many ways. Some readers will move through it from beginning to end, one chapter at a time. Others will find themselves returning repeatedly to specific sections, exercises, reflections, or tools that speak to their current challenges. Both approaches are perfectly acceptable.

As you read, we invite you to remember that this is not merely a book about sleep. It is a book about the nervous system. It is a book about healing, about the relationship between body, mind, and meaning, and most importantly, it is a book about transformation.

Throughout these pages, you will encounter stories, scientific research, practical tools, reflections, exercises, and conversations. You do not need to complete every exercise or implement every recommendation. In fact, we encourage you to resist the temptation to do everything at once.

Choose one idea, one insight, one practice, one habit, and begin there.

At the SWEET Institute, we believe that sustainable transformation occurs not through intensity but through consistency. What is repeated becomes strengthened.

You will also encounter the Four Layers of Transformation:

- The Conscious Layer, where behavior and habit change occur.
- The Pre-Conscious Layer, where beliefs, schemas, and emotional patterns are explored.
- The Unconscious Layer, where deeper emotional material is brought into awareness and integrated.
- And the Existential Layer, where questions of meaning, purpose, freedom, and identity are addressed.

As you read, notice which layer resonates most strongly with you.

You will also notice recurring references to the Biological, Psychological, Relational, Environmental, and Existential domains of experience. Sleep is never merely biological. It is shaped by every aspect of our lives.

Finally, we encourage you to read with curiosity rather than judgment. If a chapter challenges you, pause. If a reflection surprises you, explore it. If an exercise feels meaningful, repeat it. And if you find yourself becoming more compassionate toward your body and your nervous system, then the book is already doing its work.

Thank you for allowing us to accompany you on this journey.

Now take a breath. Turn the page. And let us begin.

Part I —Why We Cannot Sleep

Chapter 1 — The Exhausted World

At 2:13 in the morning, Daniel stared at the ceiling again. His body was exhausted, but his mind was not. Tomorrow's meeting replayed itself like a broken film reel: the text message he forgot to answer; the bills; the fear; the pressure; the noise; the regret; and the endless stream of unfinished thoughts moving through his nervous system like traffic that never stopped.

He reached for his phone, again; and a blue light illuminated the darkness of the room as dopamine flooded an already overstimulated brain. A quick scroll became twenty-seven minutes. Twenty-seven minutes became another layer of exhaustion; and exhaustion became frustration.

"Why can't I just sleep?" he whispered.

Across the world, millions of people ask themselves that same question every night. Some struggle to fall asleep. Some wake up repeatedly. Some wake up too early and cannot return to sleep; while others technically sleep for eight hours yet awaken feeling depleted, foggy, emotionally heavy, disconnected, and unrestored. This is not simply a sleep problem. This is a nervous system crisis.

Modern society has created conditions that continuously activate the human stress response while simultaneously demanding productivity, speed, stimulation, emotional suppression, hypervigilance, comparison, and endless accessibility. The human nervous system was never designed for this level of chronic activation.

At the SWEET Institute, we recognize that symptoms are not random failures. Symptoms are communication, and sleep difficulties are communication. The body communicates. The mind communicates. Relationships communicate. Environments communicate, and meaning systems communicate.

Insomnia is often not the problem itself. It is the visible expression of multiple deeper processes happening simultaneously across the Biological, Psychological, Relational, Environmental, and Existential domains of human experience. This is the SWEET Multi-Domain Model.

A person may say they "cannot sleep," but beneath the surface may exist elevated cortisol, unresolved grief, emotional suppression, perfectionism, trauma conditioning, loneliness, chronic overstimulation, fear of failure, existential uncertainty, alcohol dependence, attachment insecurity, digital addiction, or a nervous system that no longer associates nighttime with safety.

Many people believe sleep is simply mechanical. However, sleep is relational; sleep requires surrender; sleep requires trust; sleep requires the nervous system to temporarily release vigilance; and many people no longer feel safe enough internally to let go.

Research increasingly supports the profound connection between chronic stress, emotional dysregulation, trauma exposure, hyperarousal, and sleep disturbance. Studies demonstrate that activation of the sympathetic nervous system and dysregulation of the hypothalamic-pituitary-adrenal axis contribute significantly to insomnia and fragmented sleep patterns. Chronic hypervigilance alters sleep architecture itself, reducing restorative deep sleep and REM stability. In other words, many exhausted people are not failing to sleep because they are weak. They are exhausted because their nervous systems have adapted to survival; and survival systems do not easily power down. This is one reason traditional sleep advice often fails, "Just put the phone away." "Just relax." "Just meditate." "Just go to bed earlier."

These suggestions are not entirely wrong. In fact, many behavioral interventions are important and evidence-based. However, they often fail because they address only the conscious layer of transformation while ignoring the deeper layers underneath.

At the SWEET Institute, we understand transformation through four interconnected layers:

- **The Conscious Layer**: behaviors, routines, habits, structure, discipline, sleep hygiene, nutrition, stimulation, accountability, and lifestyle patterns.
- **The Pre-Conscious Layer**: schemas, attachment patterns, beliefs, emotional conditioning, perfectionism, fear, internal dialogue, and learned expectations.
- **The Unconscious Layer**: repressed conflicts, unresolved emotional material, defenses, symbolic communication, dreams, trauma imprints, and unintegrated emotional experiences.
- **The Existential Layer**: meaning, freedom, mortality, identity, purpose, responsibility, values, and the deeper question of how one chooses to live.

Real and lasting sleep transformation requires engagement across all four layers. This is why someone may intellectually understand sleep hygiene yet still sabotage sleep repeatedly. This is why someone may feel exhausted but continue scrolling for hours. This is also why someone may fear silence; why someone may unconsciously avoid dreams; and why some people collapse physically yet remain psychologically alert.

The issue is often deeper than information. The issue is regulation, and this book is not merely about sleep; rather, it is about restoration. It is about learning how to become physiologically regulated, psychologically safe, emotionally integrated, relationally connected, environmentally aligned, and existentially grounded.

Throughout this book, we will combine practical neuroscience, psychology, trauma research, behavioral science, mindfulness, psychodynamic understanding, attachment theory, existential reflection, and concrete implementation tools to help readers move from information to transformation, for information alone rarely changes lives. Implementation does; experience does; and embodiment does.

Therefore, the goal is not simply to teach readers how to sleep. The goal is to help readers become the kind of people whose nervous systems can finally rest; and perhaps that is one of the deepest human longings of all, and not merely sleep, but peace.

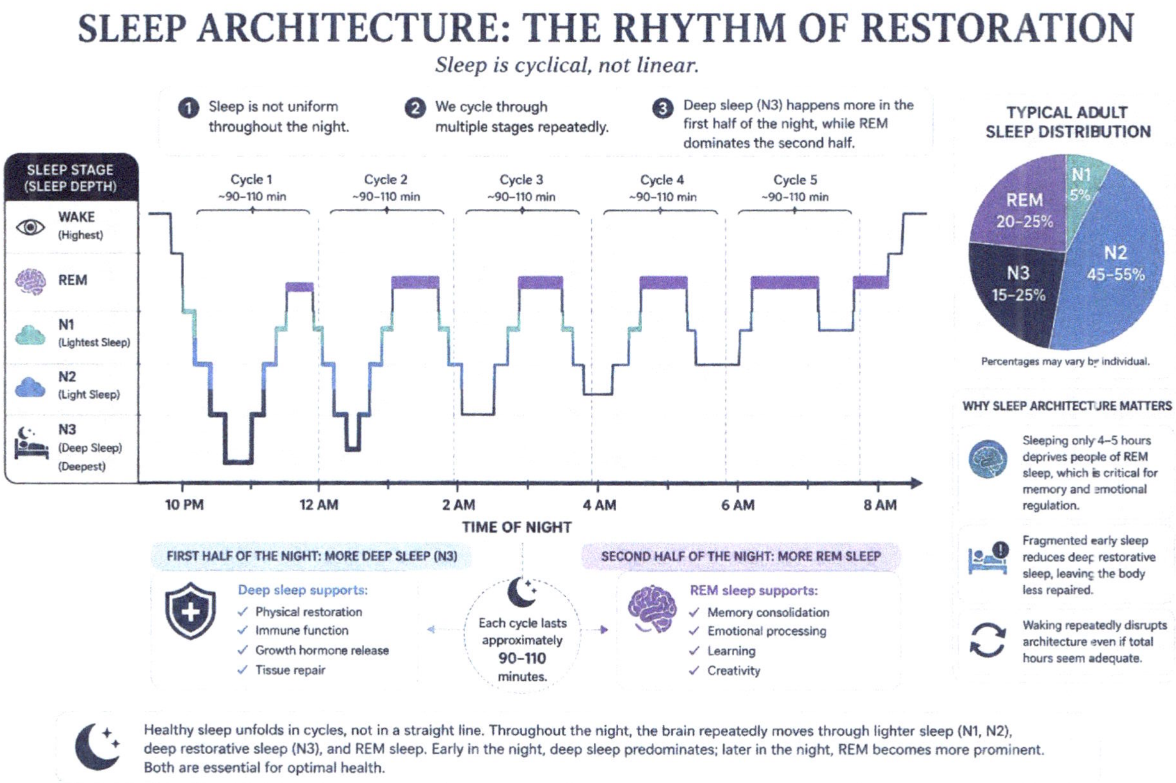

SLEEP ARCHITECTURE: THE RHYTHM OF RESTORATION
Sleep is cyclical, not linear.
1 Sleep is not uniform throughout the night.
2 We cycle through multiple stages repeatedly.
3 Deep sleep (N3) happens more in the first half of the night, while REM dominates the second half.
SLEEP STAGE (SLEEP DEPTH)
WAKE (Highest)
REM
N1 (Lightest Sleep)
N2 (Light Sleep)
N3 (Deep Sleep) (Deepest)
Cycle 1 ~90–110 min
Cycle 2 ~90–110 min
Cycle 3 ~90–110 min
Cycle 4 ~90–110 min
Cycle 5 ~90–110 min
10 PM
12 AM
2 AM
4 AM
6 AM
8 AM
TIME OF NIGHT
FIRST HALF OF THE NIGHT: MORE DEEP SLEEP (N3)
Deep sleep supports:
✓ Physical restoration
✓ Immune function
✓ Growth hormone release
✓ Tissue repair
Each cycle lasts approximately 90–110 minutes.
SECOND HALF OF THE NIGHT: MORE REM SLEEP
REM sleep supports:
✓ Memory consolidation
✓ Emotional processing
✓ Learning
✓ Creativity
TYPICAL ADULT SLEEP DISTRIBUTION
N1 5%
REM 20–25%
N2 45–55%
N3 15–25%
Percentages may vary by individual.
WHY SLEEP ARCHITECTURE MATTERS
Sleeping only 4–5 hours deprives people of REM sleep, which is critical for memory and emotional regulation.
Fragmented early sleep reduces deep restorative sleep, leaving the body less repaired.
Waking repeatedly disrupts architecture even if total hours seem adequate.
Healthy sleep unfolds in cycles, not in a straight line. Throughout the night, the brain repeatedly moves through lighter sleep (N1, N2), deep restorative sleep (N3), and REM sleep. Early in the night, deep sleep predominates; later in the night, REM becomes more prominent. Both are essential for optimal health.

Selected Scientific References

- American Academy of Sleep Medicine. (2014). *International classification of sleep disorders* (3rd ed.). American Academy of Sleep Medicine.
- Harvard Medical School Division of Sleep Medicine. (n.d.). *Understanding sleep*.
- Levine, P. A. (2010). *In an unspoken voice: How the body releases trauma and restores goodness*. North Atlantic Books.
- Perlis, M. L., Jungquist, C., Smith, M. T., & Posner, D. (2005). *Cognitive behavioral treatment of insomnia: A session-by-session guide*. Springer.
- Porges, S. W. (2011). *The polyvagal theory: Neurophysiological foundations of emotions, attachment, communication, and self-regulation*. W. W. Norton & Company.
- Siegel, D. J. (2012). *The developing mind: How relationships and the brain interact to shape who we are* (2nd ed.). Guilford Press.
- Van der Kolk, B. A. (2014). *The body keeps the score: Brain, mind, and body in the healing of trauma*. Viking.
- Walker, M. (2017). *Why we sleep: Unlocking the power of sleep and dreams*. Scribner.

Chapter 2 — Sleep Is Not Laziness

Maya had not slept well in years. She woke every morning feeling as if she had spent the entire night carrying invisible weight across invisible mountains. Her body ached, her concentration drifted, her patience shortened, coffee no longer energized her; it merely helped her survive. Yet every time she tried to rest, guilt appeared.

"If I rest, I'm lazy." "If I slow down, I'll fall behind." "Other people are doing more." "I should be stronger than this." The irony was devastating. The more exhausted she became, the more she attacked herself for being exhausted. This pattern is extraordinarily common in modern society. Many people do not merely struggle with sleep physiologically. They struggle with permission. Permission to stop. Permission to pause. Permission to be human. And, the permission to rest without shame.

At the SWEET Institute, we recognize that sleep disturbance is often not simply biological dysregulation. It is also psychological conditioning, relational learning, environmental pressure, and existential confusion unfolding simultaneously.

Many people were not raised in environments where rest felt emotionally safe. Some grew up in homes filled with chaos, unpredictability, criticism, conflict, or instability. Their nervous systems learned that nighttime was not restorative; rather, it was dangerous. Others internalized messages that productivity determined worth, and rest became associated with weakness.

Still others developed identities organized around achievement, caretaking, perfectionism, hyper-independence, or survival. For these individuals, slowing down may unconsciously trigger anxiety because motion itself became psychological protection.

This is one reason exhaustion has become normalized. Modern culture often rewards overextension while quietly punishing restoration. People brag about burnout. They glorify sleep deprivation, and wear exhaustion like a badge of importance. However, biology does not negotiate with ego. The nervous system eventually demands repayment.

Research consistently demonstrates that chronic sleep deprivation contributes to increased risk for depression, anxiety disorders, cardiovascular disease, impaired immune function, obesity, diabetes, cognitive impairment, emotional dysregulation, and decreased life expectancy. Sleep is not optional maintenance; it is foundational biological regulation.

Yet despite overwhelming evidence, many people continue treating rest as if it were earned only after complete productivity. This creates an impossible equation, the exhausted brain becomes less efficient, less emotionally regulated, less motivated, less focused, and more impulsive.

Sleep deprivation itself often worsens the very problems people attempt to solve through overworking. The exhausted person then blames themselves further, and the cycle continues.

At the conscious layer of transformation, people often need concrete behavioral restructuring around sleep. They may need consistent bedtime routines, reduction in evening stimulation, limitation of caffeine, or improved nutritional regulation. They may also need movement throughout the day, electronic boundaries, and healthier circadian alignment. These matter profoundly. However, if the deeper layers are ignored, behavioral change frequently collapses under emotional pressure.

For example, someone may intellectually know they should stop working at 7 p.m. Yet unconsciously, stopping may trigger fears of inadequacy, failure, helplessness, or loss of identity. Another person may know they should avoid nighttime scrolling. Yet psychologically, scrolling may function as emotional numbing, distraction from loneliness, avoidance of difficult thoughts, or temporary regulation for an overstimulated nervous system.

This is why information alone is insufficient. People often know what to do, so the deeper question is, "What emotional function does the unhealthy behavior serve?"

At the pre-conscious layer, many exhausted individuals carry schemas such as, "I am only valuable when productive." "If I stop, everything will fall apart." "I must always be prepared." "Rest is selfish." "Sleep is wasting time."

These beliefs shape physiology, and the body responds not merely to events, but to interpretation. A nervous system organized around chronic pressure cannot easily transition into restoration.

At the unconscious layer, deeper conflicts may emerge. Some individuals unconsciously fear stillness because stillness allows painful emotional material to surface. Others fear dreams because dreams reconnect them with grief, trauma, longing, rage, vulnerability, or unresolved memories.

For some, sleep represents surrender, and surrender feels unsafe. This is especially important for individuals with trauma histories, attachment wounds, chronic instability, or environments requiring prolonged vigilance. Their nervous systems learned adaptation through activation. Hyperarousal then became survival, and survival strategies do not disappear simply because life circumstances change. The body still remembers.

This is why healing sleep is not merely about "getting tired enough." It is about helping the nervous system relearn safety. At the existential layer, many people eventually confront an uncomfortable truth: They have built lives that continuously disconnect them from themselves, through constant stimulation, constant performance, constant urgency, and constant distraction; and underneath it all may exist profound exhaustion not only of the body, but of meaning itself.

The modern world often teaches people how to produce, but not how to rest; how to achieve, but not how to restore; and how to perform, but not how to be. True rest is not laziness. Rest is repair, regulation, integration, and biological wisdom. Rest is also psychological restoration, relational reconnection, environmental alignment, and existential recalibration. Perhaps, then, one of the greatest acts of healing in modern life is learning that your worth does not disappear the moment you become still.

Throughout this book, we will repeatedly return to a central truth: The goal is not merely to sleep more. The goal is to build a life and nervous system that no longer experiences rest as danger, for when safety returns, sleep often follows.

The Sleep Crisis

THE COST OF SLEEP DEPRIVATION

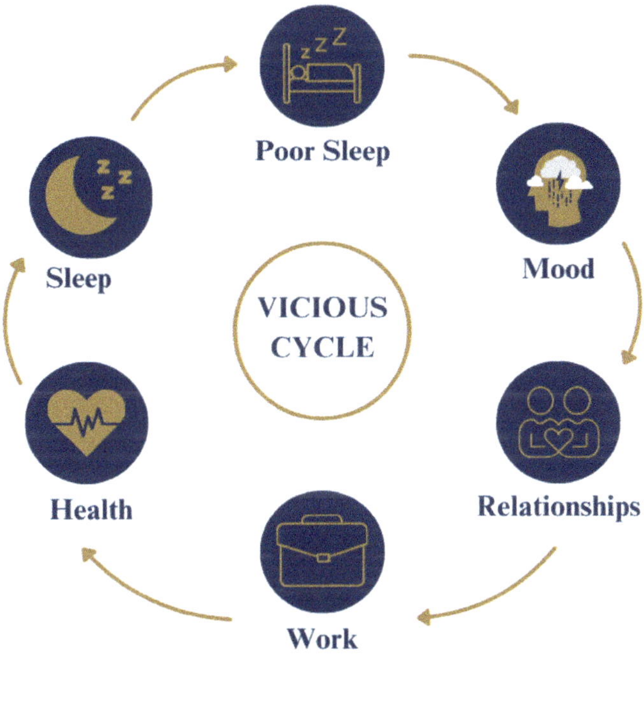

Selected Scientific References

- American Psychological Association. (n.d.). *Stress effects on the body.*
- Harvard Medical School Division of Sleep Medicine. (n.d.). *Healthy sleep.*
- Hobfoll, S. E. (1989). Conservation of resources: A new attempt at conceptualizing stress. *American Psychologist, 44*(3), 513–524.
- Perlis, M. L., Jungquist, C., Smith, M. T., & Posner, D. (2005). *Cognitive behavioral treatment of insomnia: A session-by-session guide*. Springer.
- Porges, S. W. (2011). *The polyvagal theory: Neurophysiological foundations of emotions, attachment, communication, and self-regulation.* W. W. Norton & Company.
- Siegel, D. J. (2012). *The developing mind: How relationships and the brain interact to shape who we are* (2nd ed.). Guilford Press.
- Van der Kolk, B. A. (2014). *The body keeps the score: Brain, mind, and body in the healing of trauma*. Viking.
- Walker, M. (2017). *Why we sleep: Unlocking the power of sleep and dreams*. Scribner.

Chapter 3 — The Nervous System That Forgot Safety

At 1:47 a.m., Elena sat upright in bed again. Her heart was racing, though nothing dangerous was happening in the room. The doors were locked, the apartment was quiet, and the lights from the city flickered softly against the ceiling. Still, her body behaved as if danger were inches away. She checked her phone, then the front door, then the stove, and then the clock, again, and again. She was exhausted, but her nervous system was awake.

Many people believe sleep problems begin in the mind. Yet, often, they begin in the nervous system.

At the SWEET Institute, we recognize that human beings do not merely think their way through life. They experience life through the body first, long before language, the nervous system is already scanning, interpreting, reacting, adapting, and learning.

This process occurs automatically. The body records every sound, every facial expression, and every conflict. It also records every disappointment, every loss, and every moment of unpredictability. Over time, the nervous system develops patterns.

Some nervous systems learn, "The world is mostly safe," while others learn, "Stay alert." These patterns profoundly shape sleep, and sleep, in turn, requires a temporary release of vigilance. The body must believe that it is safe enough to surrender consciousness. When the nervous system remains trapped in chronic activation, the body struggles to transition into restoration. This is why so many exhausted people describe feeling "tired but wired."

Their bodies are depleted, their nervous systems are activated, their minds are exhausted, yet their physiology remains prepared for danger. This, in essence, is adaptation.

The human nervous system evolved to protect survival. The sympathetic nervous system mobilizes the body for action during threat through increased heart rate, elevated cortisol, heightened alertness, muscular tension, and activation of stress pathways. This response is extraordinarily intelligent in moments of actual danger.

The problem emerges when the nervous system no longer knows how to return fully to safety. At that point, activation becomes chronic, and chronic activation destroys restorative sleep.

Trauma exposure, chronic stress, emotional dysregulation, attachment insecurity, adverse childhood experiences, and prolonged hypervigilance significantly alter sleep architecture and nervous system regulation. Individuals living in chronic stress states often experience reduced deep sleep, increased nighttime awakenings, elevated nighttime cortisol, fragmented REM cycles, and persistent physiological arousal.

In simple language: the body keeps preparing for danger long after the danger is over; and this is one reason sleep hygiene alone sometimes fails.

A person may, then, turn off electronics, drink herbal tea, dim the lights, and follow every recommendation correctly; yet internally, their nervous system may still be scanning for threat. This distinction changes everything.

At the conscious layer of transformation, individuals absolutely benefit from behavioral interventions, including, consistent sleep schedules, circadian alignment, movement, and nutrition. They absolutely benefit from light exposure, reduced stimulation, and structured routines.

These interventions matter, but if the deeper layers are ignored, the nervous system often overrides conscious intention. A person may desperately want sleep while simultaneously remaining physiologically activated. This is why the SWEET Institute emphasizes regulation before performance.

A dysregulated nervous system struggles to sustain behavioral change because the body must first experience safety.

At the pre-conscious layer, individuals often carry deeply conditioned expectations about the world, "I must always stay prepared." "I cannot relax." "If I let my guard down, something bad will happen." "I am responsible for everything." "Rest is dangerous." Many of these beliefs formed long before adulthood.

A child growing up in unpredictability may unconsciously learn that nighttime is unsafe. Another child may learn that emotional expression creates conflict. Another may become hyper-independent because caregivers were inconsistent or emotionally unavailable. Over time, the nervous system adapts around these experiences. Adaptation, in turn, becomes identity.

The individual may later describe themselves as "an anxious person," "a light sleeper,"

"always stressed," or "someone whose brain never shuts off." However, often, these are not personality flaws; rather, they are survival strategies that became chronic.

At the unconscious layer, even deeper material may emerge. Some individuals unconsciously fear sleep because sleep requires surrender. Others fear dreams because dreams reconnect them with unresolved emotional experiences. Some fear silence because silence allows buried thoughts and feelings to surface. Others unconsciously associate stillness with vulnerability, helplessness, or emotional exposure.

The unconscious mind continues communicating even when conscious awareness attempts to suppress distress. This is why unresolved emotional material often intensifies at night. During the day, distraction helps people avoid internal experiences. At night, stimulation decreases; silence increases; awareness expands; and the nervous system finally begins surfacing what has remained unprocessed.

This is one reason nighttime anxiety can feel so overwhelming. The mind becomes louder when distraction disappears.

At the existential layer, many individuals eventually confront a painful realization: They have spent years surviving rather than living, always preparing, always managing. always anticipating, an always protecting, but rarely resting.

Eventually the body asks, "When do we finally become safe?" This may be one of the deepest questions beneath chronic insomnia.

Instead of, "How do I force sleep?" It is, "How do I help my nervous system relearn safety?"

This shift changes the entire healing process because healing sleep is not simply about sedation. It is about restoration. It is about helping the body transition from chronic vigilance into regulated surrender; and this is where the SWEET Body–Mind–Meaning Framework becomes essential.

The body must regulate. The mind must soften; and meaning systems must reorganize. The individual must begin experiencing life differently across Biological, Psychological, Relational, Environmental, and Existential domains simultaneously.

Throughout this book, we will repeatedly explore practices that help retrain the nervous system, including breath awareness, mindfulness, body-based regulation, and emotional processing. We will also explore cognitive restructuring, attachment repair, environmental redesign, and sleep rituals, in addition to free association, dream reflection, and existential grounding.

None of these interventions work in isolation, for healing occurs through integration; so, the goal is not merely to become unconscious at night; rather, the goal is to become safe enough to rest, for deep sleep is not simply biological shutdown; rather, deep sleep is the nervous system's willingness to trust.

Circadian Rhythms

The Body Clock

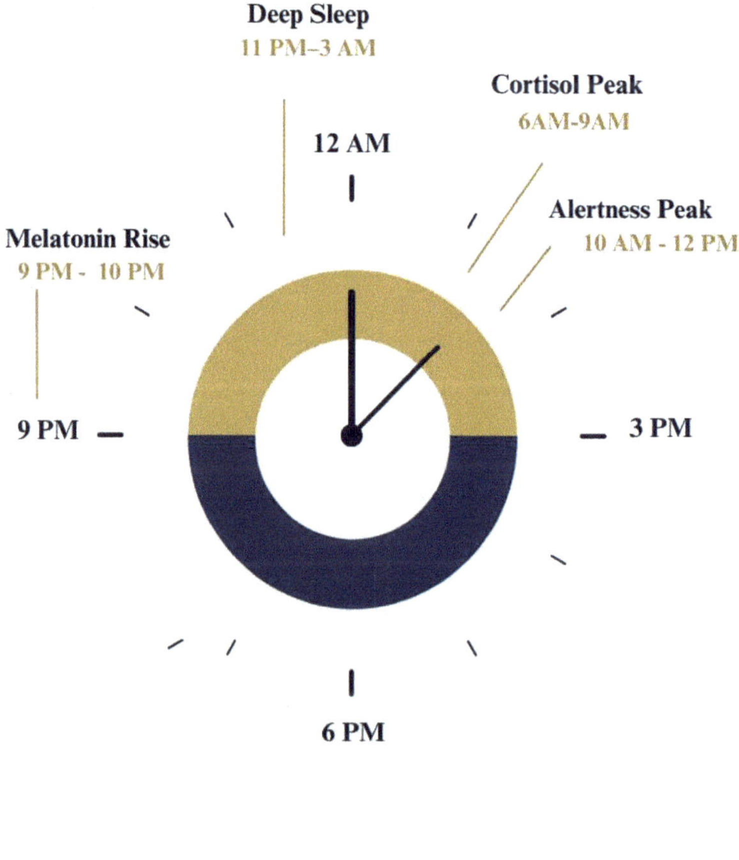

Selected Scientific References

- American Academy of Sleep Medicine. (2014). *International classification of sleep disorders* (3rd ed.). American Academy of Sleep Medicine.
- Harvard Medical School Division of Sleep Medicine. (n.d.). *Understanding the science of sleep.*
- Levine, P. A. (2010). *In an unspoken voice: How the body releases trauma and restores goodness*. North Atlantic Books.
- Porges, S. W. (2011). *The polyvagal theory: Neurophysiological foundations of emotions, attachment, communication, and self-regulation.* W. W. Norton & Company.
- Shapiro, F. (2018). *Eye movement desensitization and reprocessing (EMDR) therapy: Basic principles, protocols, and procedures* (3rd ed.). Guilford Press.
- Siegel, D. J. (2012). *The developing mind: How relationships and the brain interact to shape who we are* (2nd ed.). Guilford Press.
- Van der Kolk, B. A. (2014). *The body keeps the score: Brain, mind, and body in the healing of trauma*. Viking.
- Walker, M. (2017). *Why we sleep: Unlocking the power of sleep and dreams*. Scribner.

Chapter 4 — Hypervigilance and the Modern Mind

At 11:38 p.m., Marcus answered one final email, then another, and then another. His body was pleading for rest, but his mind remained trapped in motion. Notifications flashed, news headlines scrolled, messages accumulated, social media continued endlessly, and financial worries surfaced. Tomorrow's obligations began replaying themselves before today had even ended.

In other words, his nervous system had forgotten how to stop, and this has become one of the defining psychological realities of modern life. Human beings are now exposed to levels of stimulation, information, comparison, urgency, unpredictability, and cognitive overload that the nervous system was never designed to process continuously. The result is widespread hypervigilance.

At the SWEET Institute, we understand hypervigilance as more than anxiety. Hypervigilance is a chronic state of scanning. The nervous system continuously searches for danger, disappointment, criticism, and rejection. The nervous system also searches for uncertainty, threat, conflict, failure, loss, or emotional pain. Sometimes the apparent threats are external, but many times, the scanning becomes internalized.

People then begin monitoring themselves constantly, "How am I performing?"

"What if I fail?" "What if something goes wrong?" "What are people thinking about me?" "What if I cannot keep up?" The body remains activated long after the original dangers have passed, and eventually the nervous system begins treating ordinary life as an emergency.

This profoundly affects sleep. Sleep requires deactivation of vigilance systems, yet modern society trains the opposite, for we live in cultures of permanent alertness. Phones remain beside the bed. Work enters the bedroom. Breaking news follows people into the night; and social comparison never stops. Further, notifications interrupt nervous system recovery; artificial light disrupts circadian rhythms; productivity culture glorifies overextension; and many individuals no longer experience psychological separation between day and night. In other words, the nervous system never fully powers down.

Chronic stress exposure, excessive digital stimulation, emotional overload, trauma exposure, and persistent sympathetic nervous system activation contribute significantly to insomnia and fragmented sleep. Exposure to nighttime blue light suppresses melatonin production, while chronic cognitive stimulation increases physiological arousal and delays sleep onset.

The issue extends beyond electronics. The modern mind itself has become overstimulated, and many individuals spend the entire day consuming information without metabolizing emotional experience.

Thoughts accumulate; stress accumulates; emotions accumulate; and unprocessed experiences accumulate. Then nighttime arrives, silence emerges, and suddenly the nervous system begins surfacing everything that was emotionally postponed during the day.

This is why nighttime thinking often becomes relentless. The issue is not necessarily that the person suddenly became anxious at night. The issue is that distraction finally decreased enough for awareness to emerge.

At the conscious layer of transformation, practical behavioral interventions matter tremendously. Sleep recovery often requires reducing evening stimulation, establishing technology boundaries, limiting nighttime exposure to emotionally activating content, and creating environmental darkness. It also requires building predictable routines, improving nutrition, and reestablishing circadian rhythm consistency.

These interventions help signal safety to the body, but again, behavioral change alone often fails if deeper psychological patterns remain unaddressed.

At the pre-conscious layer, many individuals carry powerful internal beliefs that sustain hypervigilance, "I cannot relax until everything is finished." "I must stay ahead." "If I stop, I'll lose control." "Something bad is about to happen." "I need to be available at all times." Many of these schemas become reinforced by modern systems themselves.

Organizations reward overwork; social media rewards visibility; culture rewards productivity; and busyness becomes associated with importance. Eventually people confuse exhaustion with purpose, and the nervous system loses the ability to distinguish urgency from identity.

At the unconscious layer, hypervigilance often reflects unresolved emotional material. Some individuals remain psychologically activated because stillness threatens to expose grief, loneliness, rage, shame, fear, or unresolved trauma. Others unconsciously fear rest because rest creates emotional vulnerability. Hyperactivity becomes defense; distraction becomes avoidance; and constant stimulation becomes emotional anesthesia.

The unconscious mind often protects individuals from emotional pain through movement, busyness, perfectionism, or chronic activation. However, the body eventually pays the price; and this is why many exhausted people simultaneously crave rest and resist it, for a deeper part of the nervous system still associates slowing down with danger.

At the existential layer, modern hypervigilance raises painful questions about how human beings now live. Many people no longer experience true stillness. There is no silence, no darkness, or no pause. There is also, no reflection and no emotional digestion. Rather, there is only continuous stimulation, continuous noise, and continuous performance.

Yet human beings were not designed for permanent activation. The nervous system requires cycles: Activity and restoration; engagement and recovery; movement and stillness; and expression and reflection. Without these cycles, exhaustion becomes inevitable.

At the SWEET Institute, we use the SWEET SDAF Framework to help individuals interrupt dysregulated momentum:

- Stabilize.
- Decide.
- Act.
- Feel.

First stabilize the nervous system.

Then make intentional decisions.

Then engage in aligned action.

Then allow emotional integration and reflection.

Modern life often reverses this process. People act impulsively before regulating. They consume before reflecting. They react before grounding; and eventually the nervous system becomes trapped in chronic overload.

Healing sleep therefore requires more than "trying harder." It requires learning how to create internal and external conditions that support safety, regulation, emotional integration, and restoration. This may involve technology boundaries, breath awareness, mindfulness, and therapy. This may also involve attachment repair, environmental redesign, body regulation, and journaling, in addition to trauma work, dream reflection, or learning how to tolerate stillness without panic.

For healing occurs gradually, and the nervous system relearns safety through repetition: moment by moment, night by night, choice by choice; and perhaps one of the most revolutionary acts in modern society is this: To become fully present without needing constant stimulation; to sit in silence without fear; to rest without guilt; and to close the eyes without remaining psychologically at war with tomorrow.

For deep sleep is not merely about unconsciousness. Deep sleep is about finally no longer needing to remain on guard.

The Nervous System

THE REGULATION CONTINUUM

Based on Polyvagal Theory

↑ **Higher Arousal**

Fight

Hyperarousal

Threat response activated.

- Anxiety
- Panic
- Anger
- Racing thoughts

Safe & Connected

Regulated, flexible, connected.

- Calm
- Present
- Curious
- Connected

Freeze / Shutdown

Hypoarousal

Energy conservation and disconnection.

- Fatigue
- Numbness
- Disconnection
- Feeling stuck

↓ **Lower Arousal**

Selected Scientific References

- American Psychological Association. (n.d.). *Stress in America*.
- Harvard Medical School Division of Sleep Medicine. (n.d.). *Blue light has a dark side*.
- Perlis, M. L., Jungquist, C., Smith, M. T., & Posner, D. (2005). *Cognitive behavioral treatment of insomnia: A session-by-session guide*. Springer.
- Porges, S. W. (2011). *The polyvagal theory: Neurophysiological foundations of emotions, attachment, communication, and self-regulation*. W. W. Norton & Company.
- Siegel, D. J. (2012). *The developing mind: How relationships and the brain interact to shape who we are* (2nd ed.). Guilford Press.
- Twenge, J. M. (2017). *iGen: Why today's super-connected kids are growing up less rebellious, more tolerant, less happy—and completely unprepared for adulthood*. Atria Books.
- Van der Kolk, B. A. (2014). *The body keeps the score: Brain, mind, and body in the healing of trauma*. Viking.
- Walker, M. (2017). *Why we sleep: Unlocking the power of sleep and dreams*. Scribner.

Chapter 5 — The Biology of Exhaustion

Jonathan could not understand what was happening to him. He slept six hours one night, eight hours another, sometimes even nine, yet every morning, he woke feeling drained.

His body felt heavy. His concentration disappeared by midday. His patience shortened.

His motivation faded; and coffee temporarily stimulated him, while underneath the stimulation remained profound fatigue.

"What's wrong with me?" he asked.

The answer was more complex than simple tiredness.

At the SWEET Institute, we recognize that exhaustion is rarely caused by one factor alone. Exhaustion is multi-determined, emerging simultaneously across Biological, Psychological, Relational, Environmental, and Existential domains.

Many people think exhaustion simply means, "You need more sleep."

Sometimes that is true. But often, exhaustion reflects chronic nervous system dysregulation, emotional overload, inflammation, hormonal disruption, overstimulation, psychological hyperarousal, poor recovery cycles, nutritional imbalance, unresolved stress activation, trauma physiology, or lives organized around continuous depletion rather than restoration.

The body keeps score, and eventually the body demands attention, for sleep is not passive inactivity; rather, it is active biological restoration. During sleep, the body performs extraordinary functions, including memory consolidation, emotional processing, immune regulation, and hormonal balancing. It also performs cellular repair, glymphatic waste clearance, metabolic regulation, cardiovascular recovery, and nervous system recalibration.

Without adequate restorative sleep, nearly every major biological system begins to suffer. Chronic sleep deprivation contributes to increased risk of depression, anxiety, hypertension, and cardiovascular disease. It also contributes to obesity, diabetes, substance use disorders, and immune dysfunction, in addition to cognitive impairment, accidents, and decreased emotional regulation.

Even mild chronic sleep restriction significantly impairs executive functioning, attention, judgment, emotional flexibility, impulse control, and stress tolerance. The exhausted brain becomes more reactive; the exhausted body becomes more inflamed; the exhausted nervous system becomes more vulnerable to dysregulation; and eventually exhaustion begins shaping identity itself.

People begin saying, “This is just who I am.” “I’m always tired.” “My brain never works.” “I can’t focus anymore.” However, often these are not permanent character traits. They are biological consequences of chronic depletion.

At the conscious layer of transformation, biological restoration requires practical intervention. This includes consistent sleep timing, circadian rhythm alignment, movement, and nutrition. It also includes hydration, light exposure, reduction of evening stimulation, and reduced alcohol intake, in addition to management of caffeine, treatment of medical conditions, and behavioral regulation.

Instead of superficial recommendations, these are foundational biological interventions. The nervous system requires rhythm, and human physiology functions best through predictable cycles of activation and recovery. However, modern life often destroys biological rhythm.

People consume caffeine late into the day; they eat irregularly; they remain sedentary; they stare at bright screens at midnight; and they use alcohol to sedate the nervous system. They also remain psychologically activated late into the evening, and work against circadian biology rather than with it. Eventually the body loses synchronization, the nervous system becomes confused, and deep restorative sleep decreases.

One of the most misunderstood biological realities, then, is this: Sedation is not the same as restoration. Many people use substances, alcohol, medications, or overstimulation patterns that produce unconsciousness without true restorative sleep architecture. Yet a person may technically lose consciousness while still experiencing fragmented or poor-quality sleep. This distinction matters tremendously.

Deep sleep and REM sleep are essential for emotional integration, cognitive recovery, memory consolidation, and nervous system repair. Without them, the body accumulates biological debt, and at the pre-conscious layer, biology interacts continuously with psychology.

For example, chronic stress beliefs increase cortisol activation; perfectionism increases sympathetic arousal, and fear increases muscular tension. Further, shame increases inflammatory activation, and the body does not separate thought from physiology. Thoughts then become chemistry, and interpretation becomes biology.

This is why chronic anxiety frequently produces physical exhaustion. The nervous system remains mobilized continuously, and mobilization consumes energy.

At the unconscious layer, unresolved emotional material also impacts biology. Whether it be unprocessed grief, suppressed rage, chronic fear, attachment wounds, or unresolved trauma, they all influence autonomic regulation. The body then often carries emotional histories that the conscious mind no longer fully recognizes.

This is one reason trauma survivors frequently experience chronic fatigue, fragmented sleep, hyperarousal, nightmares, muscular tension, gastrointestinal distress, and nervous system dysregulation. The unconscious mind continues communicating through the body, and the body speaks in symptoms.

At the existential layer, exhaustion sometimes reflects a deeper crisis of meaning. Many individuals are biologically depleted because they are living in continuous contradiction with themselves. They have lives without boundaries, relationships without reciprocity, work without meaning, and schedules without recovery. They also have goals without alignment, and achievement without fulfillment.

Eventually the body begins protesting, since the nervous system was not designed merely to survive endless productivity, for human beings require restoration.

This is why the SWEET Body–Mind–Meaning Framework becomes essential. Healing exhaustion requires work across multiple dimensions simultaneously. The body must regulate. The mind must soften. Relationships must support safety. Environments must support restoration; and meaning systems must realign. No single intervention is sufficient alone, for healing occurs through integration.

Throughout this book, we will repeatedly explore how small consistent interventions profoundly reshape biology over time, including breath awareness, circadian alignment, body movement, and sleep rituals. These small consistent interventions also include mindfulness, emotional processing, nutrition, and trauma healing, in addition to attachment repair, environmental redesign, and nervous system regulation.

The nervous system changes through repetition instead of punishment, shame, or self-attack. It changes through compassionate, structured, repeated experiences of safety and restoration; and perhaps one of the most important truths about exhaustion is this: Your body is not betraying you; rather your body is communicating with you. It is communicating to you through the fatigue, the insomnia, the heaviness, and the inability to focus. It is also communicating with you through the irritability and the burnout.

In other words, none of these are moral failures; rather, they are signals. There are signals that the body is asking for something modern life often refuses to provide: Recovery. As such, deep sleep is not simply about getting through tomorrow; rather, deep sleep is about allowing the body to finally heal from yesterday.

Stress and Sleep

STRESS BUCKET MODEL

OVERFLOW = INSOMNIA

Selected Scientific References

- American Academy of Sleep Medicine. (n.d.). *Sleep education and clinical guidelines.*
- Harvard Medical School Division of Sleep Medicine. (n.d.). *Healthy sleep resources.*
- Perlis, M. L., Jungquist, C., Smith, M. T., & Posner, D. (2005). *Cognitive behavioral treatment of insomnia: A session-by-session guide*. Springer.
- Porges, S. W. (2011). *The polyvagal theory: Neurophysiological foundations of emotions, attachment, communication, and self-regulation.* W. W. Norton & Company.
- Sapolsky, R. M. (2004). *Why zebras don't get ulcers* (3rd ed.). Holt Paperbacks.
- Siegel, D. J. (2012). *The developing mind: How relationships and the brain interact to shape who we are* (2nd ed.). Guilford Press.
- Van der Kolk, B. A. (2014). *The body keeps the score: Brain, mind, and body in the healing of trauma*. Viking.
- Walker, M. (2017). *Why we sleep: Unlocking the power of sleep and dreams*. Scribner.

Chapter 6 — The Hidden Cost of Sleeplessness

Sophia did not realize how much sleep deprivation had changed her. She thought she was simply "stressed," but gradually, her life began shrinking. Her patience with her children decreased; her emotional reactions intensified; and her concentration deteriorated. Her motivation also disappeared; her relationships felt heavier; small problems felt enormous; joy became harder to access; and even hope felt more distant. Yet, because exhaustion had become normal, she barely recognized how profoundly her nervous system had changed; and this is one of the most dangerous aspects of chronic sleep deprivation. People adapt to impairment.

At the SWEET Institute, we recognize that sleeplessness does not remain confined to the night. Sleep deprivation quietly affects every domain of human functioning: biological, psychological, relational, environmental, and existential.

Sleep disruption changes how people think, how they feel, how they interpret reality, and how they connect. It also changes how they regulate, how they hope, and eventually, how they experience themselves.

The modern world often minimizes this reality, and people are taught to "push through," "Keep grinding," "Stay productive," "Sleep when you're dead." However, the nervous system cannot endlessly override biology without consequence, and eventually the cost emerges.

Chronic sleep deprivation significantly impacts emotional regulation, executive functioning, memory consolidation, decision-making, immune functioning, metabolic health, cardiovascular functioning, and psychological resilience. Even modest sleep restriction increases irritability, impulsivity, anxiety sensitivity, emotional reactivity, and cognitive distortion, for the exhausted brain interprets reality differently.

When people are sleep deprived, threat perception increases, frustration tolerance decreases, negative emotional bias intensifies, and cognitive flexibility declines. In simple terms: everything feels harder. The exhausted nervous system becomes more reactive because it has fewer internal resources available for regulation. This affects relationships profoundly.

At the relational domain of the SWEET Multi-Domain Model, chronic exhaustion often decreases patience, empathy, emotional presence, communication quality, and capacity for connection. People become shorter with loved ones, more emotionally reactive, less tolerant, and more avoidant. They also become more withdrawn or r more emotionally explosive. This is because exhausted nervous systems struggle to regulate, and this is one reason sleeplessness often creates secondary suffering. The individual not only feels exhausted internally, but they begin experiencing relational consequences externally. Conflict increases, isolation increases, misunderstandings increase, and shame increases; and shame itself further disrupts nervous system regulation.

At the conscious layer of transformation, many people underestimate how much seemingly "small" habits accumulate biologically over time. A few hours lost nightly; late-night scrolling; irregular schedules; and constant stimulation. They then develop into alcohol before bed, poor nutrition, sedentary behavior, and chronic stress.

Individually these may seem manageable, but together they gradually destabilize biological restoration, and because deterioration happens slowly, people often fail to notice the progression, until burnout arrives, or panic attacks, or depression, or emotional collapse, or cognitive fog severe enough to disrupt daily functioning.

At the pre-conscious layer, chronic exhaustion frequently intensifies negative core beliefs. The exhausted mind becomes more vulnerable to thoughts such as, "I can't handle this." "I'm failing." "Everything is too much." "I'll never get better."

Sleep deprivation decreases psychological resilience, and even manageable stressors begin feeling overwhelming. This is why insomnia and mood disorders often reinforce one another. Poor sleep worsens emotional regulation; poor emotional regulation worsens sleep; and the cycle feeds itself.

At the unconscious layer, chronic sleeplessness sometimes reflects unresolved emotional activation that the body continues carrying automatically. Suppressed grief; fear; hypervigilance; and trauma, in addition to attachment insecurity, and chronic emotional suppression. The body does not simply "forget" emotional experiences because conscious awareness moves on. The nervous system remembers, and often, the more emotionally overloaded the system becomes, the more restorative sleep deteriorates.

The unconscious mind continues communicating through dreams, physiological arousal, muscular tension, and nighttime activation.

At the existential layer, prolonged exhaustion can create profound disconnection from meaning itself. Exhausted people often stop asking, "What matters?" They begin asking only, "How do I survive the day?" Then, life narrows, creativity decreases, presence decreases, wonder decreases, and connection decreases; and the individual gradually becomes trapped in functional survival.

This is one reason chronic exhaustion is not merely physical depletion. It is often existential depletion. People stop feeling fully alive. The world becomes gray; and because this change often happens slowly, many individuals mistakenly believe they have "lost themselves." However, often, the nervous system has simply remained deprived of restoration for too long.

This is why healing sleep is not superficial self-care. Healing sleep restores access to:

clarity, emotional flexibility, patience, and motivation. It also restores access to memory, creativity, hope, and connection. The body begins recovering; the mind begins softening; the nervous system begins regulating; and the individual begins returning to themselves.

At the SWEET Institute, we repeatedly emphasize this central principle: Symptoms are communication; exhaustion communicates; brain fog communicates; irritability communicates; and insomnia communicates. The body is not trying to punish people; rather, the body is trying to protect survival. However, protection without recovery eventually becomes suffering.

Throughout this book, we will explore practical strategies to reverse this cycle across all four layers of transformation, including behavioral change, nervous system regulation, schema restructuring, emotional processing, unconscious integration, and existential realignment, remembering that healing occurs through consistency, instead of perfection.

In other words, the nervous system changes through repeated experiences of safety, rhythm, restoration, and integration; and perhaps one of the most important truths about sleeplessness is this: Many people are not lazy, weak, or failing; rather, they are exhausted beyond what their nervous systems were ever designed to sustain; and healing begins the moment exhaustion stops being treated as a personal flaw and starts being understood as a signal, for deep sleep is not simply about feeling less tired; rather, deep sleep is about reclaiming life from survival.

Technology and Sleep

THE EVENING STIMULATION LADDER

Selected Scientific References

- American Psychological Association. (n.d.). *Stress in America.*
- Harvard Medical School Division of Sleep Medicine. (n.d.). *Sleep and mental health resources.*
- Perlis, M. L., Jungquist, C., Smith, M. T., & Posner, D. (2005). *Cognitive behavioral treatment of insomnia: A session-by-session guide*. Springer.
- Porges, S. W. (2011). *The polyvagal theory: Neurophysiological foundations of emotions, attachment, communication, and self-regulation.* W. W. Norton & Company.
- Sapolsky, R. M. (2004). *Why zebras don't get ulcers* (3rd ed.). Holt Paperbacks.
- Siegel, D. J. (2012). *The developing mind: How relationships and the brain interact to shape who we are* (2nd ed.). Guilford Press.
- Van der Kolk, B. A. (2014). *The body keeps the score: Brain, mind, and body in the healing of trauma*. Viking.
- Walker, M. (2017). *Why we sleep: Unlocking the power of sleep and dreams*. Scribner.

Part II – The Conscious Layer

Chapter 7 — Rebuilding the Sleep Window

At 12:42 a.m., Darren told himself he would go to sleep in "just ten more minutes." Ten minutes became forty-five; forty-five became another episode; another episode became scrolling; scrolling became online shopping; and suddenly it was 2:11 a.m., again.

The next morning, he blamed himself, "I have no discipline." However, the reality was more complicated.

At the SWEET Institute, we recognize that many people are not merely struggling with sleep. They are struggling with rhythm. The human nervous system was designed around cycles: light and darkness; activation and restoration; movement and stillness; and focus and recovery. Modern life disrupts these rhythms continuously; artificial light extends daytime into midnight; and phones remove psychological separation between work and rest.

Further, stress delays nervous system deactivation; inconsistent schedules confuse circadian biology; overstimulation delays melatonin release; and emotional overload keeps the body activated long after the day has ended. Eventually the body loses its natural sleep rhythm; and this is where rebuilding the sleep window becomes essential.

The "sleep window" refers to the body's natural period of physiological readiness for sleep. When people repeatedly override this window through stimulation, work, electronics, stress, or irregular schedules, the nervous system gradually loses synchronization with its own biological timing. The body becomes confused; and people often describe this as, "I'm exhausted all day but awake at night."

This pattern is extraordinarily common in modern society.

At the biological domain of the SWEET Multi-Domain Model, circadian rhythm disruption profoundly affects hormonal regulation, cortisol patterns, melatonin production, mood stability, energy regulation, cognitive functioning, metabolism, and emotional resilience.

The nervous system depends on predictability, and predictability creates safety. Maintaining relatively consistent sleep and wake times improves sleep quality, emotional regulation, circadian stability, and overall physiological restoration. Exposure to natural morning light helps regulate melatonin and cortisol rhythms, while irregular sleep schedules increase biological dysregulation and insomnia symptoms.

However, rebuilding the sleep window is not only biological; it is also psychological.

At the conscious layer of transformation, many individuals need practical restructuring around nighttime behavior. This includes consistent wake times, evening light reduction, limiting late-night stimulation, and decreasing screen exposure. This also includes reducing caffeine intake, establishing sleep rituals, creating calming transitions, and allowing the body repeated opportunities to relearn rhythm.

One of the most important principles in sleep restoration is this: The wake time matters more than the bedtime. Many people attempt to "catch up" on sleep by sleeping at dramatically inconsistent times. Unfortunately, this often further destabilizes circadian rhythm regulation, for the body learns through repetition, while consistency helps retrain biological timing systems.

Morning light exposure becomes especially important because it helps anchor circadian rhythm through regulation of melatonin and cortisol cycles. Even brief exposure to natural outdoor light early in the day can significantly improve nighttime sleep quality over time.

Movement also matters profoundly. Human physiology evolved for physical activity. Sedentary living contributes to nervous system dysregulation, metabolic disruption, muscular tension, inflammation, and impaired sleep pressure accumulation. Regular movement throughout the day helps the body distinguish activation periods from restoration periods. However, rebuilding the sleep window requires more than behavior alone.

At the pre-conscious layer, many individuals unknowingly sabotage nighttime regulation through emotional patterns. Some fear tomorrow; some avoid nighttime because it forces confrontation with loneliness; some experience bedtime as the only personal time they control, leading to “revenge bedtime procrastination,” where individuals delay sleep to reclaim autonomy after emotionally exhausting days.

Others associate nighttime with stress because years of insomnia conditioned the bed itself into an anxiety trigger. The mind then begins anticipating failure before sleep even starts. Thoughts emerge automatically, “What if I can’t sleep again?” “What if tomorrow is ruined?” “I need to force myself to sleep.”

Ironically, effort itself often increases arousal, for sleep cannot be forced; rather, sleep emerges through conditions. This distinction changes everything.

At the unconscious layer, nighttime may activate unresolved emotional material that remained suppressed during the day. Silence reduces distraction; awareness increases; and the nervous system begins surfacing thoughts, feelings, memories, fears, or conflicts that daytime activity helped avoid. This is one reason many people suddenly feel emotionally flooded at night.

The issue is not necessarily that nighttime "creates" anxiety. The issue is that nighttime removes enough stimulation for previously unprocessed material to become noticeable. This is why nervous system regulation must include emotional integration. The goal, then, is not merely sedation; rather, the goal is helping the body feel safe enough to surrender.

At the existential layer, rebuilding the sleep window often requires rebuilding the relationship with time itself. Many individuals live in constant urgency, always rushing, always reacting, always producing, and always anticipating. The nervous system never receives clear signals that the day has truly ended; and this is why rituals matter, for rituals communicate transition.

A nighttime routine tells the body, "We are safe now." "The day is complete." "It is time to release." Simple practices repeated consistently become powerful regulatory signals. These include dim lighting, warm showers, stretching, and breath awareness. These also include journaling, soft music, reading, gratitude reflection, as well as mindfulness, or calming conversation. These are not trivial habits. They are nervous system language.

At the SWEET Institute, we often emphasize this truth: The body learns safety through repetition, instead of intensity, perfection, self-criticism, or repetition. Night after night, the nervous system slowly relearns regulation, and this process requires compassion.

Many individuals attack themselves aggressively around sleep, "I'm failing again." "What's wrong with me?" "I'll never fix this." However, self-attack itself activates the nervous system further. Healing then requires a different relationship with the body, for the body is not the enemy; rather, the nervous system is trying to adapt.

Throughout this book, we will continue building practical frameworks for restoring rhythm across all five domains of human experience: the biological, the psychological, the relational, the environmental, and the existential, for deep sleep is not merely about exhaustion finally overpowering the body; rather, deep sleep emerges when the nervous system relearns rhythm, predictability, and trust.

Sleep Hygiene

Deep Sleep Checklist

MORNING	AFTERNOON	EVENING	NIGHT
☐ Wake at a consistent time.	☐ Stay physically active.	☐ Reduce screen exposure (1–2 hours before bed).	☐ Keep bedroom cool, dark, and quiet.
☐ Get 10–20 minutes of natural light.	☐ Limit caffeine after early afternoon.	☐ Eat a lighter evening meal.	☐ Put devices away.
☐ Hydrate.	☐ Manage stress with short breaks.	☐ Dim lights.	☐ Practice a calming bedtime ritual.
☐ Move your body.	☐ Avoid long naps.	☐ Journal or reflect.	☐ Go to bed during your natural sleep window.

Selected Scientific References

- American Academy of Sleep Medicine. (n.d.). *Sleep hygiene recommendations*.
- Harvard Medical School Division of Sleep Medicine. (n.d.). *Healthy sleep habits*.
- Huberman, A. (2021). *Toolkit for sleep. Huberman Lab Podcast*.
- Perlis, M. L., Jungquist, C., Smith, M. T., & Posner, D. (2005). *Cognitive behavioral treatment of insomnia: A session-by-session guide*. Springer.
- Porges, S. W. (2011). *The polyvagal theory: Neurophysiological foundations of emotions, attachment, communication, and self-regulation*. W. W. Norton & Company.
- Siegel, D. J. (2012). *The developing mind: How relationships and the brain interact to shape who we are* (2nd ed.). Guilford Press.
- Walker, M. (2017). *Why we sleep: Unlocking the power of sleep and dreams*. Scribner.
- Walker, W. H., II, Walton, J. C., DeVries, A. C., & Nelson, R. J. (2020). Circadian rhythm disruption and mental health. *Translational Psychiatry, 10*(1), 28.

Chapter 8 — The Bedroom as a Nervous System Environment

At 12:18 a.m., Natalie walked into her bedroom carrying stress from the entire day. The television was already on; notifications continued flashing across her phone; laundry covered the chair in the corner; and work documents sat open on the desk.

The room itself felt restless, and somehow, without realizing it, she had trained her nervous system to associate the bedroom not with restoration, but with activation.

At the SWEET Institute, we recognize that environments shape physiology. Human beings are constantly responding to cues, including light, sound, temperature, and clutter. We are also constantly to smell, noise, visual stimulation, emotional associations, and relational experiences. The nervous system continuously asks, "Am I safe here?"

Most people think of the bedroom as merely a physical space, yet psychologically and biologically, the bedroom becomes a conditioned nervous system environment. Over time, the body learns associations. If the bedroom repeatedly becomes linked with stress, conflict, work, or scrolling, the nervous system begins anticipating wakefulness there automatically. The same is true if the bedroom repeatedly becomes linked with fear, insomnia, overstimulation, or emotional activation, for the body learns patterns.

This is why many individuals report feeling sleepy while watching television in another room, only to suddenly feel wide awake the moment they enter bed. The bed itself has become associated with performance pressure and frustration.

At the biological domain of the SWEET Multi-Domain Model, environmental conditions strongly influence circadian rhythm regulation, melatonin production, autonomic activation, and sleep architecture. In other words, temperature matters; lighting matters; noise matters; and air quality matters, in addition to comfort and sensory input.

Cooler temperatures, darkness, reduced noise exposure, and minimized stimulation significantly improve sleep quality and restorative sleep duration. Exposure to artificial light, particularly blue-spectrum light, suppresses melatonin and delays sleep onset. The nervous system responds to environment continuously; and this is why the bedroom should ideally become one of the most regulating spaces in a person's life.

At the conscious layer of transformation, rebuilding the bedroom environment often requires practical restructuring. This includes reducing clutter, limiting electronics, darkening the room, and maintaining cooler temperatures. This also includes using comfortable bedding, decreasing stimulation, minimizing noise, and creating predictable sensory cues associated with calmness and restoration.

Many individuals underestimate the impact of visual clutter. Clutter communicates unfinished tasks, and unfinished tasks maintain cognitive activation. The nervous system struggles to fully release when the environment continuously signals incompletion.

This does not mean perfection is required. It means the environment should support exhalation rather than vigilance.

Lighting is especially important. Human circadian biology evolved around sunlight and darkness. Artificial light exposure late at night confuses biological timing systems, decreases melatonin release, and delays sleep readiness. One of the simplest and most powerful interventions is dimming environmental light approximately one to two hours before bedtime. This communicates transition. Warm lighting, softer sensory input, and reduced stimulation help signal safety to the body.

Temperature also matters profoundly. The body naturally lowers core temperature during sleep initiation. Excessive warmth disrupts this process and often fragments sleep architecture.

The nervous system sleeps best when the environment supports physiological downregulation. However, environmental regulation is not merely physical.

At the psychological domain, emotional associations profoundly shape sleep experiences. If someone repeatedly experiences panic attacks in bed, the body may begin associating bedtime with fear. If someone frequently argues with a partner before sleep, the bedroom may become emotionally activating. If someone works nightly in bed, the nervous system may stop distinguishing between performance space and restoration space. The body learns context; and this is why rebuilding sleep often requires rebuilding association.

At the pre-conscious layer, many individuals unknowingly maintain environmental conditions that reinforce dysregulation. Some remain surrounded by stimulation because silence feels emotionally uncomfortable. Others sleep with televisions on because stillness activates loneliness. Some constantly consume information late into the night because distraction protects them from difficult emotional experiences. The environment often reflects deeper psychological needs.

At the unconscious layer, the bedroom may carry symbolic meaning. For some, nighttime evokes vulnerability. For others, isolation. For others, grief. For trauma survivors, darkness itself may activate implicit memory systems associated with danger. This is why "simple sleep advice" sometimes fails. The nervous system is responding not only to the room itself, but to emotional history associated with the room. Healing requires integration across all layers.

At the existential layer, the modern bedroom has increasingly become invaded by productivity culture. Work enters the bed; stress enters the bed; news enters the bed; conflict enters the bed; and social comparison enters the bed.

The space once associated with restoration becomes psychologically colonized by performance; and eventually the nervous system no longer knows where recovery begins.

At the SWEET Institute, we often encourage individuals to ask a simple question, "What does my bedroom communicate to my nervous system?" Does it communicate: urgency,

stimulation, unfinished pressure, and vigilance? Or does it communicate: safety, slowness, predictability, softness, and permission to release the day?

In other words, small changes matter. A lamp instead of overhead lighting; a charging station outside the bed; a calming scent; and a clean sheet. It might also be a ritualized cup of tea; gentle music; breath awareness; a journal; or simply silence. The nervous system responds to repeated cues; and this is why rituals become powerful, for rituals transform spaces, and repeated calming experiences slowly retrain the body's associations with nighttime and rest.

The body learns, "This place is safe." "This is where we restore." "This is where we release." Over time, the nervous system begins anticipating sleep rather than fearing it.

Throughout this book, we will continue exploring how environmental regulation interacts with body regulation, emotional integration, relational safety, and existential restoration.

Deep sleep does not emerge only from exhaustion; rather, deep sleep emerges from environments, both internal and external, that teach the nervous system it no longer has to remain on guard.

Thoughts and Sleep

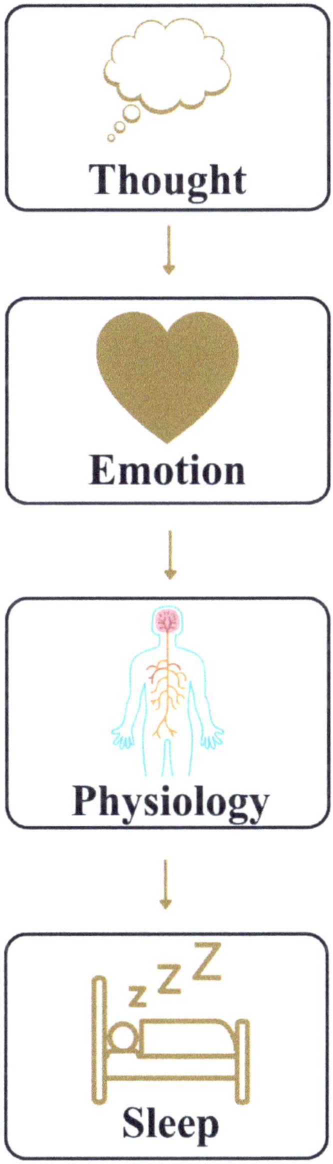

Selected Scientific References

- American Academy of Sleep Medicine. (n.d.). *Sleep hygiene recommendations*.
- Harvard Medical School Division of Sleep Medicine. (n.d.). *Healthy sleep environment guidelines*.
- Perlis, M. L., Jungquist, C., Smith, M. T., & Posner, D. (2005). *Cognitive behavioral treatment of insomnia: A session-by-session guide*. Springer.
- Porges, S. W. (2011). *The polyvagal theory: Neurophysiological foundations of emotions, attachment, communication, and self-regulation*. W. W. Norton & Company.
- Siegel, D. J. (2012). *The developing mind: How relationships and the brain interact to shape who we are* (2nd ed.). Guilford Press.
- Van der Kolk, B. A. (2014). *The body keeps the score: Brain, mind, and body in the healing of trauma*. Viking.
- Walker, M. (2017). *Why we sleep: Unlocking the power of sleep and dreams*. Scribner.
- Walker, W. H., II, Walton, J. C., DeVries, A. C., & Nelson, R. J. (2020). Circadian rhythm disruption and mental health. *Translational Psychiatry, 10*(1), 28.

Chapter 9 — Caffeine, Alcohol, Nicotine, and Sleep

At 9:45 p.m., Andre poured himself another drink. He told himself it helped him relax, and in some ways, it did. His shoulders softened. His thoughts slowed slightly, and the emotional pressure of the day became quieter.

For a brief moment, his nervous system felt relief, but around 2:17 a.m., he woke up again. His heart was racing. His mouth was dry. His sleep felt shallow, and his mind immediately reactivated.

The next morning, he felt exhausted, again.

At the SWEET Institute, we recognize that many individuals unknowingly use substances and stimulation patterns in attempts to regulate dysregulated nervous systems. They use caffeine, or alcohol, nicotine, or sugar. They may also use late-night eating, energy drinks, scrolling, or overworking.

Often these are not merely "bad habits." They are attempts at nervous system management.

The issue is that many of these strategies temporarily relieve discomfort while simultaneously worsening long-term regulation and sleep quality.

At the biological domain of the SWEET Multi-Domain Model, substances profoundly affect circadian rhythms, neurotransmitter systems, autonomic activation, hormonal regulation, sleep architecture, and nervous system recovery.

Many people misunderstand how dramatically these substances impact restorative sleep. Caffeine, for example, is one of the most socially normalized stimulants in the world. It temporarily blocks adenosine receptors, reducing the sensation of fatigue and increasing alertness. However, the body continues accumulating biological sleep pressure underneath the stimulation.

The result is often a mismatch: the individual feels temporarily awake while the nervous system becomes progressively more depleted. Caffeine, for example, can remain active in the body for many hours after consumption. Even afternoon caffeine intake may significantly delay sleep onset, reduce deep sleep quality, and fragment restorative sleep architecture in sensitive individuals.

Many exhausted people enter a cycle of fatigue, caffeine, temporary stimulation, sleep disruption, more fatigue, then more caffeine. Eventually the nervous system loses rhythm.

Alcohol presents a different but equally important problem. Many people believe alcohol "helps" sleep because it increases sedation. However, sedation is not the same as restoration.

Alcohol frequently fragments sleep architecture, suppresses REM sleep, increases nighttime awakenings, worsens breathing disturbances, destabilizes autonomic regulation, and increases early-morning activation. The individual may fall asleep faster while simultaneously receiving poorer quality restorative sleep. This creates one of the most dangerous illusions in sleep health: confusing unconsciousness with healing.

Nicotine similarly increases nervous system activation through stimulation of dopamine and adrenaline pathways. While some individuals experience temporary calming effects through smoking rituals or behavioral association, nicotine itself increases physiological arousal and disrupts restorative sleep processes.

Late-night eating can also affect sleep quality through metabolic activation, reflux symptoms, blood sugar fluctuations, digestive stress, and circadian disruption. The body struggles to fully transition into restoration while simultaneously performing significant digestive processing.

At the conscious layer of transformation, improving sleep often requires direct behavioral awareness around these patterns. This does not mean perfection. It means honesty.

Many individuals underestimate how much caffeine they consume, how late they consume it, how dependent the nervous system has become on stimulation, or how much alcohol and nicotine are masking deeper dysregulation. Awareness becomes the first step toward change.

At the pre-conscious layer, substances often become linked with emotional coping patterns. Coffee may symbolize productivity and identity. Alcohol may symbolize emotional escape, reward, relaxation, or permission to stop performing. Nicotine may symbolize regulation, grounding, familiarity, or emotional containment. Food may symbolize comfort, safety, distraction, or soothing.

This is why behavioral change is rarely just behavioral. People are not simply removing substances. They are often losing coping systems. This is why shame-based approaches frequently fail.

The deeper question is, "What emotional function is this substance serving?"

At the unconscious layer, substances may help suppress emotional experiences that feel overwhelming. Grief, loneliness, fear, or trauma. They also may be suppressing shame, anger, emptiness, or hypervigilance. The nervous system often seeks immediate regulation through externally driven methods when internal regulation feels inaccessible.

This does not mean people are weak. It means the nervous system is attempting adaptation. However, adaptation through stimulation or sedation eventually creates biological debt, and the body always keeps the account.

At the existential layer, modern society continuously reinforces chemically driven activation.

Wake up quickly. Perform constantly. Stay productive, or stay stimulated. Push through exhaustion. It may also take the form of reward yourself with sedation at night, and repeat tomorrow.

In this case, the nervous system becomes trapped between stimulation and collapse. True restoration, then, requires something deeper. The body needs rhythm. The mind needs slowing. The nervous system needs safety. The individual needs recovery rather than temporary escape.

At the SWEET Institute, we often emphasize that sustainable healing requires replacing dysregulating patterns with regulating alternatives rather than relying solely on deprivation. For example, morning light instead of excess caffeine, movement instead of stimulation, breath awareness instead of impulsive reactivity, connection instead of emotional isolation, ritual instead of sedation, mindfulness instead of automatic coping, restoration instead of collapse. The nervous system changes gradually, and small repeated shifts accumulate biologically over time.

This could be a slightly earlier caffeine cutoff; reduced alcohol frequency; more hydration; consistent meals; and morning sunlight. This could also be evening calming rituals, or gentler transitions into sleep. These changes may initially seem small, but biology responds to consistency, and consistency creates regulation.

Throughout this book, we will continue exploring how healing sleep requires interventions across all layers of transformation: behavioral, psychological, unconscious,

and existential.

Deep sleep does not emerge from overpowering the body with stimulation or sedation. It emerges when the nervous system no longer needs artificial methods to force activation or escape exhaustion, and when the body finally relearns balance.

Selected Scientific References

- American Academy of Sleep Medicine. (n.d.). *Sleep hygiene and substance use guidelines*.
- Harvard Medical School Division of Sleep Medicine. (n.d.). *Effects of stimulants and alcohol on sleep*.
- National Institute on Alcohol Abuse and Alcoholism. (n.d.). *Alcohol and sleep*.
- Perlis, M. L., Jungquist, C., Smith, M. T., & Posner, D. (2005). *Cognitive behavioral treatment of insomnia: A session-by-session guide*. Springer.
- Porges, S. W. (2011). *The polyvagal theory: Neurophysiological foundations of emotions, attachment, communication, and self-regulation*. W. W. Norton & Company.
- Roehrs, T., & Roth, T. (2008). Caffeine: Sleep and daytime sleepiness. *Sleep Medicine Reviews, 12*(2), 153–162. https://doi.org/10.1016/j.smrv.2007.07.004
- Van der Kolk, B. A. (2014). *The body keeps the score: Brain, mind, and body in the healing of trauma*. Viking.
- Walker, M. (2017). *Why we sleep: Unlocking the power of sleep and dreams*. Scribner.

Chapter 10 — Electronics, Dopamine, and Revenge Bedtime Procrastination

At 1:06 a.m., Jasmine was still scrolling. She had told herself she would go to sleep an hour ago, yet somehow one video became another, one message became another, one article became another, and one notification became another.

Her body was exhausted, her eyes burned, yet she could not stop. Beneath the scrolling was a painful truth she barely recognized: This was the only time of day that felt like hers.

At the SWEET Institute, we recognize that many nighttime behaviors are not simply failures of discipline. They are attempts to reclaim emotional needs that were neglected throughout the day. This is one reason revenge bedtime procrastination has become increasingly common in modern society.

Revenge bedtime procrastination refers to delaying sleep despite exhaustion because nighttime becomes associated with autonomy, freedom, emotional decompression, stimulation, distraction, or recovery from emotionally overwhelming days.

The individual knows sleep is needed, but psychologically, staying awake feels emotionally necessary. This is a matter of communication.

At the biological domain of the SWEET Multi-Domain Model, electronics profoundly impact nervous system regulation, circadian biology, dopamine systems, emotional processing, and sleep architecture.

Phones, social media platforms, streaming systems, games, and digital environments are intentionally designed to capture attention through variable reward systems that continuously stimulate dopamine pathways. Novelty activates the brain; unpredictability activates the brain; and notifications activate the brain.

The nervous system remains alert because the next piece of information might provide emotional reward, distraction, validation, excitement, relief, or escape. Nighttime electronic exposure delays melatonin production increases cognitive arousal, fragments sleep quality, and decreases restorative deep sleep. Blue-spectrum light exposure suppresses circadian signaling, while emotionally stimulating content maintains sympathetic nervous system activation. However, the issue extends far beyond blue light. The deeper issue is psychological overstimulation. Modern humans rarely experience uninterrupted stillness. The moment discomfort appears; distraction becomes available instantly. Loneliness? Scroll. Anxiety? Watch something. Boredom? Refresh the feed. Sadness? Consume more stimulation.

The nervous system never fully metabolizes emotional experience because stimulation continually interrupts awareness.

At the conscious layer of transformation, behavioral boundaries around electronics become essential for sleep restoration. This often includes removing phones from the bed, setting technology cutoffs, reducing nighttime notifications, and using dim lighting.

This also includes creating screen-free wind-down periods and replacing stimulation with regulating rituals.

These interventions matter tremendously, but behavioral advice alone frequently fails because the behavior itself serves deeper emotional functions.

At the pre-conscious layer, many individuals unconsciously use electronics to regulate unmet psychological needs.

Some use stimulation to avoid loneliness. Some use endless information consumption to manage uncertainty. Some seek validation through social media engagement. Others use scrolling to avoid difficult thoughts, emotions, memories, or existential discomfort.

Many people experience nighttime as the only time they are no longer performing for others. Throughout the day they work, care give, respond, and produce. The also manage, perform, and survive. Nighttime becomes the first moment of emotional autonomy; and this is why people often resist sleep even while exhausted, for sleep represents surrendering the only remaining personal space they feel they control.

At the unconscious layer, electronics sometimes function as defenses against emotional contact. Silence allows awareness. Awareness may allow grief. Grief may allow vulnerability. Vulnerability may activate fear; and so, stimulation continues.

The unconscious mind often prefers distraction over emotional exposure, but the nervous system pays the price. Continuous stimulation prevents emotional integration, and the brain never fully completes recovery cycles.

Attention becomes fragmented. The body remains activated, and the mind remains noisy. Eventually the individual feels both overstimulated and emotionally disconnected simultaneously.

At the existential layer, the modern world has created unprecedented competition for human attention. Attention has become an economy, and entire industries profit from keeping nervous systems activated. The result is that many people no longer experience true psychological endings to the day. In other words, there is no natural closure; rather, there is only continuous consumption, continuous comparison, and continuous stimulation.

The nervous system never receives the message, "The day is complete." This is why intentional rituals become revolutionary.

At the SWEET Institute, we emphasize that the nervous system requires transition. The body needs signals that activity is ending and restoration is beginning. This may include dimming lights, placing the phone outside the bedroom, stretching, or breath awareness. This may also include journaling, gratitude reflection, gentle music, meditation, reading, or emotionally grounding conversation.

These practices are not simply "sleep hacks." They are nervous system communication, for repeated calming rituals slowly retrain the body's expectations around nighttime. The nervous system begins learning, "We no longer need stimulation to survive."

One of the most important shifts in healing sleep is this: The goal is not merely removing electronics. The goal is helping individuals become capable of being present without needing constant distraction. This is difficult for many people because stillness initially reveals emotional overload that stimulation previously concealed.

However, healing requires contact. Contact with the body, the mind, emotion, silence, meaning, and self. This is where the SWEET Body–Mind–Meaning Framework becomes essential. The body must downregulate. The mind must soften. Meaning systems must reorganize around restoration rather than constant consumption. The nervous system slowly relearns that rest does not equal emptiness. Rest equals recovery.

Throughout this book, we will continue exploring how modern overstimulation fragments nervous system regulation and how intentional practices restore rhythm, safety, emotional integration, and deep restorative sleep. Deep sleep is not simply the absence of wakefulness. It is what emerges when the nervous system no longer needs endless stimulation to avoid itself.

Selected Scientific References

- Alter, A. (2017). *Irresistible: The rise of addictive technology and the business of keeping us hooked.* Penguin Press.
- American Academy of Sleep Medicine. (n.d.). *Sleep hygiene recommendations.*
- Harvard Medical School Division of Sleep Medicine. (n.d.). *Blue light has a dark side.*
- Perlis, M. L., Jungquist, C., Smith, M. T., & Posner, D. (2005). *Cognitive behavioral treatment of insomnia: A session-by-session guide.* Springer.
- Porges, S. W. (2011). *The polyvagal theory: Neurophysiological foundations of emotions, attachment, communication, and self-regulation.* W. W. Norton & Company.
- Twenge, J. M. (2017). *iGen: Why today's super-connected kids are growing up less rebellious, more tolerant, less happy—and completely unprepared for adulthood.* Atria Books.
- Van der Kolk, B. A. (2014). *The body keeps the score: Brain, mind, and body in the healing of trauma.* Viking.
- Walker, M. (2017). *Why we sleep: Unlocking the power of sleep and dreams.* Scribner.

Chapter 11 — Breath Awareness and the Sleeping Body

At 2:04 a.m., Leah laid in bed trying desperately to force herself to sleep. The harder she tried, the more awake she became. Her chest felt tight. Her jaw remained tense. Her thoughts accelerated. Her breathing became shallow and fast. And without realizing it, her body was communicating something important: The nervous system did not feel safe.

At the SWEET Institute, we recognize that the body and mind are not separate systems operating independently. Thoughts affect physiology; physiology affects thoughts; emotion affects breathing; and breathing affects emotion. The body continuously communicates with the nervous system, and one of the most powerful communication systems available to human beings is breath.

Most people barely notice their breathing throughout the day. Yet breathing patterns profoundly shape autonomic regulation, emotional activation, stress responses, muscular tension, cardiovascular functioning, and sleep readiness. The breath becomes a bridge between body and mind.

At the biological domain of the SWEET Multi-Domain Model, chronic stress often produces physiological activation patterns characterized by shallow breathing, increased muscular tension, elevated heart rate, sympathetic nervous system activation, and decreased parasympathetic recovery. The body prepares for danger, even when no immediate danger exists. The nervous system shifts into survival mode, and survival physiology does not easily transition into restorative sleep.

This is why so many exhausted people describe feeling, “tired but wired.” The body is exhausted. The nervous system is activated. Breath awareness becomes powerful because it directly influences autonomic regulation.

Slow, intentional breathing stimulates parasympathetic nervous system activation through pathways closely connected to vagal regulation. Breath-focused practices reduce physiological arousal, improve emotional regulation, decrease anxiety, and support sleep quality by helping the nervous system transition from mobilization into restoration.

At the SWEET Institute, breath awareness is not merely a relaxation technique. It is a relationship; A relationship with the body, a relationship with awareness, and a relationship with presence.

At the conscious layer of transformation, many individuals benefit from practical breath awareness practices integrated into bedtime routines. Simple interventions matter; slowing the exhale, softening the jaw, relaxing the shoulders, and breathing through the nose. They also include lengthening exhalation, and intentionally reducing physiological activation before sleep.

One especially important principle is this: The exhale communicates safety. Longer exhalations help downregulate sympathetic activation and signal to the nervous system that immediate survival mobilization is no longer necessary. The body begins receiving the message, “We can release now.”

This is why many calming breath practices emphasize slower exhalation rather than aggressive inhalation. Sleep does not emerge from forcing activation. Sleep emerges from allowing release.

At the psychological domain, breath awareness also interrupts cognitive spiraling. When individuals become trapped in loops of worry, catastrophizing, rumination, or performance anxiety around sleep. Attention becomes consumed by future-focused thinking. The nervous system remains activated because the mind continues simulating danger. Breath awareness gently redirects attention back toward embodied presence.

At the pre-conscious layer, many individuals unknowingly carry breathing patterns shaped by years of stress, trauma, perfectionism, anxiety, or hypervigilance. Some chronically hold their breath. Some breathe shallowly throughout the day. Some remain physically braced without awareness. Over time, the body learns chronic contraction; and chronic contraction prevents deep restoration.

This is why many people initially struggle with stillness and breath awareness practices. The moment slowing begins, awareness increases, and awareness may expose emotional overload that distraction previously concealed.

At the unconscious layer, breath awareness sometimes reconnects individuals with emotional experiences stored beneath conscious awareness: Grief, Fear, Loneliness., Sadness, Longing, and Anger. The body often carries emotional history through muscular tension, autonomic activation, and physiological guarding. As regulation increases, previously disconnected emotional material may gradually surface.

At the existential layer, breathing reconnects individuals with a profound reality often forgotten in modern life: Human beings are not machines. They are living organisms that are rhythmic, embodied, emotional, and relational.

The modern world often trains people to live disconnected from bodily awareness entirely. People rush, consume, react, perform, stimulate, and produce. Eventually they stop listening to the body, yet the body never stops communicating. The body whispers first, then symptoms emerge, then exhaustion, then burnout, then collapse. Breath awareness becomes one way of returning home to the body before collapse becomes necessary.

At the SWEET Institute, we emphasize that breath awareness is not about perfection. People often approach mindfulness practices with the same performance mindset that dysregulated them initially, “I’m doing it wrong.” “My mind won’t stop.” “I can’t relax.” The goal is not perfect stillness; rather, the goal is relationship. Returning attention gently, repeatedly, and compassionately, for the nervous system learns safety through repetition.

This is why even brief moments of intentional breathing throughout the day accumulate biologically over time. It may be a pause before entering the home, a slow exhale before sleep, a moment of grounding after conflict, or a breath before reacting impulsively. Small moments reshape nervous system regulation gradually.

Throughout this book, we will continue integrating breath awareness into broader systems of sleep restoration: environmental regulation, behavioral restructuring, emotional integration, trauma healing, mindfulness, attachment repair, and existential grounding. For deep sleep is not merely the shutting down of consciousness; rather, it is what emerges when the body finally receives permission to release vigilance; and often, the breath becomes the first doorway back to that permission.

Selected Scientific References

- Brown, R. P., & Gerbarg, P. L. (2005). Sudarshan Kriya yogic breathing in the treatment of stress, anxiety, and depression: Part I—Neurophysiologic model. *The Journal of Alternative and Complementary Medicine, 11*(1), 189–201.
- Harvard Medical School Division of Sleep Medicine. (n.d.). *Relaxation techniques for better sleep.*
- Kabat-Zinn, J. (1990). *Full catastrophe living: Using the wisdom of your body and mind to face stress, pain, and illness*. Dell Publishing.
- Perlis, M. L., Jungquist, C., Smith, M. T., & Posner, D. (2005). *Cognitive behavioral treatment of insomnia: A session-by-session guide*. Springer.
- Porges, S. W. (2011). *The polyvagal theory: Neurophysiological foundations of emotions, attachment, communication, and self-regulation*. W. W. Norton & Company.
- Siegel, D. J. (2012). *The developing mind: How relationships and the brain interact to shape who we are* (2nd ed.). Guilford Press.
- Van der Kolk, B. A. (2014). *The body keeps the score: Brain, mind, and body in the healing of trauma*. Viking.
- Walker, M. (2017). *Why we sleep: Unlocking the power of sleep and dreams*. Scribner.

Chapter 12 — The Power of Ritual and Routine

Every night at 10:30 p.m., Olivia told herself she wanted peace. However, her evenings told a different story. Some nights she worked until exhaustion. Some nights she scrolled endlessly. Some nights she ate late. Some nights she fell asleep with the television on. Some nights she answered emails in bed. Some nights she stayed awake simply because she dreaded tomorrow.

Her body never knew what to expect, and eventually, her nervous system stopped trusting nighttime altogether.

At the SWEET Institute, we recognize that the nervous system depends profoundly on rhythm, predictability, and repetition. Human beings are pattern-based organisms. The body learns through repeated experience. The mind learns through repeated interpretation. The nervous system learns through repeated states. This is why rituals matter. Rituals communicate safety, transition, predictability; and predictability helps calm the nervous system.

Modern life often destroys ritual. People move through their days reactively: waking abruptly, consuming stimulation immediately, rushing constantly, multitasking continuously, working irregularly, and collapsing into sleep without emotional decompression or physiological transition. The nervous system never fully exits activation mode.

There is no clear beginning, no clear ending, no emotional digestion, and no slowing. There is only continuous momentum, but the body was not designed for endless momentum. The nervous system requires cycles.

At the biological domain of the SWEET Multi-Domain Model, rituals help regulate circadian rhythms, autonomic functioning, hormonal signaling, emotional regulation, and sleep readiness. Repeated behavioral patterns gradually become physiological cues.

The body begins anticipating what comes next, and this is one reason children often sleep better with structured bedtime routines. Predictability decreases uncertainty, and decreased uncertainty lowers nervous system activation.

Adults need ritual too. Consistent bedtime routines improve sleep quality, decrease sleep latency, reduce stress activation, and strengthen circadian rhythm stability. Repeated calming behaviors gradually become conditioned signals that support parasympathetic activation and physiological downregulation. However, rituals are not merely behavioral systems. They are emotional communication.

At the conscious layer of transformation, many individuals benefit enormously from intentionally creating nighttime routines that support slowing, regulation, and transition.

This does not require perfection; rather, it requires consistency. Simple repeated actions become powerful nervous system language. They include dimming lights, washing the face, stretching, and drinking tea. They also include reading, journaling, breath awareness, and gratitude reflection, in addition to gentle music, soft conversation, or silence.

These actions repeatedly communicate, "The day is ending." "We are slowing now." "We are safe enough to release." The nervous system learns through repetition; yet one of the most important mistakes people make is waiting until they are "ready" to create routine. However, routine itself creates readiness, and the body stabilizes through structure.

This becomes especially important for individuals whose lives contain chronic unpredictability, trauma histories, emotional dysregulation, or overwhelming schedules. Ritual creates containment.

At the psychological domain, rituals also help reduce cognitive overload. Modern minds remain flooded with unfinished tasks, emotional residue, digital stimulation, and anticipatory thinking. Without intentional decompression, the nervous system carries the entire day directly into bed. Ritual interrupts momentum. It creates psychological closure. This is why reflective practices become so powerful before sleep.

Journaling, for example, helps externalize mental overload rather than forcing the nervous system to hold everything internally overnight. Breath awareness helps shift attention from cognitive activation into embodied regulation. Gratitude practices gently redirect attention away from chronic threat scanning. The nervous system begins transitioning from vigilance into restoration.

At the pre-conscious layer, rituals often reshape emotional associations with nighttime itself. Many individuals unconsciously associate bedtime with failure, anxiety, loneliness, or pressure. They also associate it with rumination, or insomnia. Repeated calming rituals gradually create new emotional conditioning. The body slowly learns, “Nighttime no longer means danger.”

This process takes time. The nervous system changes through repetition rather than intensity.

At the unconscious layer, rituals also create emotional containment. Human beings have always used rituals to process uncertainty, transition, grief, fear, hope, and vulnerability. Nighttime itself is psychologically symbolic. It represents ending, surrender, stillness, loss of control, and temporary unconsciousness.

For some individuals, these experiences unconsciously activate fear. Ritual softens the transition. It creates emotional holding. This is one reason rituals often feel deeply regulating even when simple. The nervous system experiences continuity.

At the existential layer, ritual reconnects individuals with intentional living. Modern society increasingly encourages impulsivity, overstimulation, and fragmentation.

Ritual restores consciousness. Instead of collapsing unconsciously into exhaustion, the individual begins intentionally preparing for restoration. This changes the relationship with sleep entirely.

Sleep stops becoming a battle, a collapse, or a desperate escape.

Sleep becomes a return, a release, and a transition into restoration.

At the SWEET Institute, we often emphasize that rituals are not about rigid control. They are about compassionate structure. Many individuals approach routines with perfectionistic intensity, "If I miss one night, I failed." However, nervous system healing does not require perfection. It requires repetition that is gentle, compassionate and sustainable.

Further, even small rituals matter. It might be a consistent wake time; five minutes of breath awareness; lower lighting; or a warm shower. It might also be short reflection, a calming playlist, or brief moment of stillness. The body remembers patterns, and over time, these patterns begin reshaping physiology itself. The nervous system starts anticipating calm instead of anticipating stimulation. The body begins releasing tension more easily. Sleep pressure aligns more naturally, and restoration deepens.

Throughout this book, we will continue exploring how healing sleep requires rebuilding rhythm across behavioral, psychological, relational, unconscious, and existential domains simultaneously. Deep sleep is not simply something that "happens." It is often the result of repeated rituals that slowly teach the nervous system, "We no longer need to stay prepared for danger." "We are finally allowed to rest."

Selected Scientific References

- American Academy of Sleep Medicine. (n.d.). *Sleep hygiene recommendations*.
- Harvard Medical School Division of Sleep Medicine. (n.d.). *Healthy sleep habits*.
- Kabat-Zinn, J. (1990). *Full catastrophe living: Using the wisdom of your body and mind to face stress, pain, and illness*. Dell Publishing.
- Perlis, M. L., Jungquist, C., Smith, M. T., & Posner, D. (2005). *Cognitive behavioral treatment of insomnia: A session-by-session guide*. Springer.
- Porges, S. W. (2011). *The polyvagal theory: Neurophysiological foundations of emotions, attachment, communication, and self-regulation*. W. W. Norton & Company.
- Siegel, D. J. (2012). *The developing mind: How relationships and the brain interact to shape who we are* (2nd ed.). Guilford Press.
- Van der Kolk, B. A. (2014). *The body keeps the score: Brain, mind, and body in the healing of trauma*. Viking.
- Walker, M. (2017). *Why we sleep: Unlocking the power of sleep and dreams*. Scribner.

Chapter 13 — Stabilize → Decide → Act → Feel

At 11:52 p.m., Kevin was standing in front of the refrigerator again. He was not hungry, but his body felt restless. His mind felt overloaded. His chest felt tight. His nervous system felt agitated. Part of him wanted to sleep. Another part wanted relief, and without fully realizing it, he was searching for regulation.

At the SWEET Institute, we recognize that many behaviors people judge harshly in themselves are actually attempts at nervous system management. Late-night eating, scrolling, drinking, and smoking. Overthinking, working, watching television, gaming, and impulsive shopping are additional ones.

Often, these behaviors are not random. They are efforts, sometimes unconscious efforts, to shift emotional and physiological states. This is why the SWEET SDAF Framework becomes so important:

Stabilize → Decide → Act → Feel.

Most people reverse the sequence. They feel overwhelmed. They act impulsively. Then they experience consequences. Then they feel shame. The nervous system remains dysregulated. The cycle repeats. Yet healing sleep requires interruption of automatic cycles, and interruption begins with regulation.

At the biological domain of the SWEET Multi-Domain Model, dysregulated nervous systems struggle to make intentional decisions consistently. When individuals are chronically activated, exhausted, stressed, inflamed, emotionally overloaded, or sleep deprived, the brain shifts increasingly toward survival-based functioning.

Impulsivity increases. Emotional reactivity increases. Decision quality decreases. Threat perception increases. Short-term coping becomes prioritized over long-term restoration. Emotional dysregulation and chronic stress impair executive functioning, reduce impulse control, increase compulsive coping behaviors, and weaken the nervous system's ability to sustain intentional behavioral change.

This is why so many individuals know what they "should" do around sleep but struggle to implement it consistently. Knowledge alone does not regulate the nervous system.

At the conscious layer of transformation, the first task becomes learning how to regulate before making decisions.

This changes everything.

Instead of, "I'm anxious, so let me scroll."

The sequence becomes, "I notice activation. Let me regulate first."

Then comes breathing, stretching, grounding, and pausing. Also comes hydrating, walking, softening the body, and educing stimulation. Then comes the final decision. The regulated nervous system makes different choices than the dysregulated nervous system.

This is why emotional states matter so profoundly. Many unhealthy nighttime behaviors occur not because people lack intelligence, but because they are attempting to make decisions while physiologically overwhelmed. The body is activated; the mind is flooded; the nervous system wants immediate relief; and immediate relief often overrides long-term restoration.

At the psychological domain, regulation creates space between impulse and action. Without regulation, behaviors become automatic; the individual reacts rather than chooses; and this is why awareness itself becomes transformative. A pause interrupts momentum, and often, healing begins inside the pause.

At the pre-conscious layer, many individuals carry deeply conditioned emotional patterns around nighttime. Some associate nighttime with dread; some fear tomorrow; some fear silence; and some unconsciously experience stillness as unsafe.

The nervous system automatically seeks distraction, stimulation, or sedation because activation feels intolerable. However, regulation increases tolerance.

The body slowly learns, "We can survive stillness." "We can experience emotion without escaping immediately." "We can remain present without collapsing." This process reshapes nervous system flexibility.

At the unconscious layer, many nighttime behaviors function defensively.

Some people scroll to avoid grief; some eat to avoid emptiness; some drink to avoid emotional exposure; some overwork to avoid vulnerability; and some remain busy because stillness threatens to surface unresolved emotional material.

The unconscious mind continuously attempts to protect the individual from psychological pain. Yet protection through chronic avoidance often prevents restoration; and the nervous system remains trapped in activation. This is why the SWEET SDAF Framework is not simply behavioral; rather, it is transformational, for regulation creates the possibility of conscious choice, and without stabilization, survival patterns dominate automatically.

At the existential layer, the modern world encourages chronic reactivity, instant stimulation, instant access, instant distraction, and instant consumption.

People rarely pause long enough to notice their internal state before acting. However, healing sleep requires intentional slowing.

The nervous system must relearn transition. One of the most important shifts in this process is recognizing that feelings themselves are not dangerous.

Many people spend years attempting to escape discomfort rather than learning how to move through it safely. However, emotions are physiological experiences. They rise, they peak, they shift, and they move.

The nervous system becomes more resilient when individuals stop treating every uncomfortable feeling as an emergency requiring immediate avoidance.

This is where the final step of the SDAF Framework becomes essential: Feel instead of collapsing into emotion and instead of becoming overwhelmed by emotion. Allow emotional experience to move through awareness without immediate escape; and this changes the relationship with nighttime profoundly.

The body no longer needs endless stimulation to suppress internal experience, and the nervous system gradually becomes capable of rest.

At the SWEET Institute, we often emphasize that healing sleep is not simply about forcing better habits. It is about creating internal conditions where healthy choices become more emotionally accessible. This is why compassion matters.

Many individuals attack themselves constantly, “Why can’t I stop?” “What’s wrong with me?” “I know better.” However, shame itself dysregulates the nervous system further.

Healing then requires a different approach: Notice, pause, regulate, and then decide. The nervous system changes through repetition, and one regulated pause at a time.

Throughout this book, we will continue applying the SWEET SDAF Framework to sleep restoration, emotional stabilization, nervous system healing, and behavioral transformation across all four layers of transformation, for deep sleep is not merely about controlling behavior. It emerges when the nervous system no longer has to react automatically to every wave of discomfort; and it emerges when regulation becomes stronger than impulse.

Selected Scientific References

- Kabat-Zinn, J. (1990). *Full catastrophe living: Using the wisdom of your body and mind to face stress, pain, and illness*. Dell Publishing.
- Linehan, M. M. (2015). *DBT skills training manual* (2nd ed.). Guilford Press.
- Perlis, M. L., Jungquist, C., Smith, M. T., & Posner, D. (2005). *Cognitive behavioral treatment of insomnia: A session-by-session guide*. Springer.
- Porges, S. W. (2011). *The polyvagal theory: Neurophysiological foundations of emotions, attachment, communication, and self-regulation*. W. W. Norton & Company.
- Sapolsky, R. M. (2004). *Why zebras don't get ulcers* (3rd ed.). Holt Paperbacks.
- Siegel, D. J. (2012). *The developing mind: How relationships and the brain interact to shape who we are* (2nd ed.). Guilford Press.
- Van der Kolk, B. A. (2014). *The body keeps the score: Brain, mind, and body in the healing of trauma*. Viking.
- Walker, M. (2017). *Why we sleep: Unlocking the power of sleep and dreams*. Scribner.

Part III – The Pre-Conscious Layer

Chapter 14 — The Internal Dialogue That Keeps Us Awake

At 1:31 a.m., Rachel was physically in bed. However, psychologically, she was everywhere else. Her mind replayed conversations from years ago. She imagined future disasters, criticized unfinished tasks, reviewed mistakes, prepared defenses, and predicted failure. Beneath all the thinking was a quieter voice she rarely questioned, "You are not safe."

At the SWEET Institute, we recognize that many people are not simply kept awake by external stressors. They are kept awake by the internal dialogue continuously shaping their nervous systems.

Human beings live not only in environments. They live inside interpretations. The body responds not merely to events, but to the meaning attached to those events. This is why two people can experience the same situation while their nervous systems respond completely differently. The mind is constantly generating narratives about the self, about the future, about danger, and about worth. The mind is also constantly generating narratives about failure, about control, about love, and about safety.

Over time, these narratives become physiological experiences. Thoughts become chemistry, and interpretation becomes biology.

At the psychological domain of the SWEET Multi-Domain Model, internal dialogue profoundly shapes emotional regulation, stress activation, sleep quality, autonomic functioning, attention patterns, and nervous system recovery. The mind continuously communicates with the body.

A thought such as, "I'll never be okay," may immediately increase muscular tension, heart rate, cortisol activation, and sympathetic nervous system arousal. The nervous system reacts as though danger is present. This becomes especially important at night.

During the day, distraction often masks internal dialogue. We have work, noise, conversations, and tasks. We also have movement, and stimulation, but nighttime removes many distractions. Silence increases, and suddenly the internal world becomes louder.

This is why so many individuals report, "My brain won't shut off." Yet often, the issue is not excessive thinking alone. The issue is the emotional tone of the thinking; and many individuals unknowingly carry internal dialogues organized around threat, criticism, hyper-responsibility, and fear. They also carry internal dialogues around shame, or perfectionism.

In other words, the nervous system remains activated because the mind continues simulating danger. Research consistently demonstrates that rumination, chronic worry, catastrophic thinking, perfectionism, and negative repetitive thought patterns significantly contribute to insomnia, hyperarousal, anxiety, and emotional dysregulation. Persistent cognitive activation delays nervous system downregulation and interferes with restorative sleep onset.

At the conscious layer of transformation, individuals benefit from learning how to recognize and interrupt dysregulating thought patterns. Awareness becomes foundational for most people automatically believe every thought that appears in consciousness, yet thoughts are not always truth.

Thoughts are often predictions, associations, conditioning, and learned fears. They are also often protective strategies, or unresolved emotional echoes. This distinction changes everything. A thought such as, "What if tomorrow goes badly?" does not necessarily require immediate physiological mobilization.

However, the nervous system often reacts automatically before conscious awareness intervenes. This is why mindfulness-based practices become so important. Mindfulness helps individuals observe thoughts without automatically fusing with them. The goal is not suppressing thought; rather, the goal is changing the relationship to thought.

At the pre-conscious layer, internal dialogue frequently reflects deeper schemas formed through earlier relational experiences. A child repeatedly criticized may internalize, "I'm never enough." A child raised in unpredictability may internalize, "I must always stay prepared." A child exposed to emotional inconsistency may internalize, "Something bad is always about to happen."

These beliefs often continue operating automatically long into adulthood. The individual may not consciously choose them. The nervous system simply learned them through repetition; and because the mind repeats these narratives continuously, the body begins experiencing them as reality.

At the unconscious layer, internal dialogue sometimes serves defensive functions. Catastrophic thinking may create the illusion of preparation. Self-criticism may unconsciously attempt to prevent rejection. Overthinking may function as protection against uncertainty; and hyper-analysis may protect against emotional vulnerability.

The unconscious mind often believes constant thinking increases safety. However, the nervous system pays the price. The body remains activated, sleep deteriorates, and restoration decreases. Eventually the person becomes trapped in chronic internal vigilance.

At the existential layer, many individuals unknowingly organize entire lives around fear-based internal narratives. Always preparing, always proving, always anticipating, and always defending. The nervous system never receives permission to release, yet healing requires a profound shift: The mind must stop treating every uncertainty as an emergency.

At the SWEET Institute, we often encourage individuals to begin asking different questions at night. Instead of "How do I force sleep?" We ask, "What is my internal dialogue communicating to my nervous system right now?"

Is the mind communicating danger, urgency, failure, pressure, or catastrophe? Or is it communicating safety, permission, compassion, flexibility, and trust?

Small shifts matter, and the nervous system listens continuously to internal language. Individuals can start learning to replace, "I'll never sleep." with, "My nervous system is activated right now, and activation can change;" or replace, "I'm failing." with, "My body is asking for support;" or replace, "I have to control everything." with, "I can allow uncertainty without collapsing."

Compassionate internal dialogue does not eliminate difficulty instantly, but it changes physiology gradually. This is why cognitive restructuring, mindfulness, schema work, acceptance practices, journaling, and emotional awareness become essential components of sleep healing, for chronic internal threat signaling dysregulates the nervous system continuously, and healing requires changing the emotional environment inside the mind itself.

Throughout this book, we will continue exploring how thoughts, emotions, bodily states, relationships, and unconscious patterns interact to shape sleep and restoration across all four layers of transformation, for deep sleep is not simply about silence in the room; rather, it often begins when the mind itself no longer sounds like danger.

The Two Inner Voices

The Fear Voice

Survival Mode

Reactive
Catastrophic
Rigid
Urgent
Defensive
Perfectionistic
Hypervigilant

"You won't sleep."

"Tomorrow is ruined."

"You're not safe."

The Wise Voice

Regulated Self

Grounded
Compassionate
Flexible
Reflective
Accepting
Patient
Regulated

"You are activated, not broken."

"This moment will pass."

"Your body can learn safety."

Fear Voice vs. Wise Voice

Two ways of interpreting the same experience

Situation	Fear Voice	Wise Voice
Can't fall asleep	*"Something is wrong."*	*"My body is activated right now."*
Awake at 3 a.m.	*"Tomorrow is ruined."*	*"One difficult night is manageable."*
Racing thoughts	*"I must stop thinking."*	*"I can observe thoughts without fighting them."*
Anxiety	*"I'm losing control."*	*"My nervous system is trying to protect me."*
Mistake during the day	*"I failed."*	*"I'm human and still learning."*
Uncertainty	*"I need certainty now."*	*"I can tolerate not knowing everything."*
Exhaustion	*"I'll never get better."*	*"Healing is gradual and possible."*

Listening for the Wise Voice

Which voice is speaking right now?

☐ Fear Voice ☐ Wise Voice

What would the Wise Voice say instead?

Selected Scientific References

- Beck, A. T. (1976). *Cognitive therapy and the emotional disorders*. International Universities Press.
- Hayes, S. C., Strosahl, K. D., & Wilson, K. G. (2016). *Acceptance and commitment therapy: The process and practice of mindful change* (2nd ed.). Guilford Press.
- Kabat-Zinn, J. (1990). *Full catastrophe living: Using the wisdom of your body and mind to face stress, pain, and illness*. Dell Publishing.
- Perlis, M. L., Jungquist, C., Smith, M. T., & Posner, D. (2005). *Cognitive behavioral treatment of insomnia: A session-by-session guide*. Springer.
- Porges, S. W. (2011). *The polyvagal theory: Neurophysiological foundations of emotions, attachment, communication, and self-regulation*. W. W. Norton & Company.
- Siegel, D. J. (2012). *The developing mind: How relationships and the brain interact to shape who we are* (2nd ed.). Guilford Press.
- Walker, M. (2017). *Why we sleep: Unlocking the power of sleep and dreams*. Scribner.
- Young, J. E., Klosko, J. S., & Weishaar, M. E. (2003). *Schema therapy: A practitioner's guide*. Guilford Press.

Chapter 15 — Perfectionism Never Sleeps

At 12:57 a.m., Daniel was mentally rehearsing tomorrow again: the presentation, the wording, the timing, and the possible mistakes. He was also rehearsing the imagined criticism, the backup plans, and the backup plans for the backup plans.

His body was exhausted, but his mind refused to release control. "If I can just think through everything enough," he told himself, "maybe nothing will go wrong."

Yet nothing ever felt fully finished. Nothing ever felt fully safe, and sleep became impossible.

At the SWEET Institute, we recognize that perfectionism is often misunderstood. Many people think perfectionism is simply about high standards. However, psychologically, perfectionism is often about fear. It's about fear of failure, fear of rejection, fear of criticism, and fear of shame. It's also about fear of not being enough.

The perfectionistic nervous system remains chronically activated because it experiences mistakes not merely as inconveniences, but as threats to identity, worth, belonging, or emotional safety. This profoundly affects sleep, for sleep requires surrender, and perfectionism resists surrender.

At the psychological domain of the SWEET Multi-Domain Model, perfectionism often creates chronic internal pressure, hypervigilance, overthinking, anticipatory anxiety, emotional rigidity, and difficulty disengaging from cognitive activity.

The mind continuously scans, "What did I miss?" "What if I fail?" "What if I disappoint someone?" "What if I lose control?" The nervous system remains mobilized because the internal world continuously communicates that safety depends on flawless performance.

This creates exhaustion, and paradoxically, the more exhausted the individual becomes, the more perfectionistic control often intensifies. Research consistently demonstrates strong associations between perfectionism, anxiety disorders, insomnia, chronic stress, emotional dysregulation, burnout, and depressive symptoms. Perfectionistic thinking increases cognitive arousal, rumination, physiological activation, and sleep-onset difficulties. The perfectionistic mind rarely rests.

At the conscious layer of transformation, many individuals recognize the behavioral consequences of perfectionism, including overworking, overpreparing, difficulty stopping, late-night productivity, and constant checking. They also include reassurance-seeking, and inability to disengage mentally from unfinished tasks.

However, behavioral awareness alone often fails to create lasting change because perfectionism is rarely rooted only in behavior. It is rooted in emotional conditioning.

At the pre-conscious layer, perfectionistic individuals often carry deeply internalized beliefs such as, "If I make mistakes, I will be rejected." "My worth depends on performance." "I must always stay ahead." "If I relax, everything will fall apart." "Being imperfect is dangerous." Many of these beliefs develop early in life.

Children raised in environments characterized by criticism, unpredictability, emotional inconsistency, high expectations, conditional approval, or instability often learn that achievement increases emotional safety. The nervous system adapts, and over time, perfectionism becomes not simply a strategy, but an identity.

The person no longer knows how to feel safe without constant striving. This is why many perfectionistic individuals struggle intensely with nighttime stillness. During the day, achievement creates temporary distraction and structure. At night, stillness removes performance, and without performance, unresolved fears often surface.

At the unconscious layer, perfectionism frequently functions defensively. Perfectionism may defend against shame, against helplessness, against vulnerability, against grief, and against feelings of inadequacy.

The unconscious mind believes, "If I can control everything perfectly enough, maybe I can avoid emotional pain." However, this creates chronic nervous system activation, for the body never fully releases vigilance, and the individual remains psychologically "on call" even while physically exhausted.

This is one reason perfectionistic people often experience difficulty falling asleep, difficulty staying asleep, nighttime rumination, and muscular tension. They also experience jaw clenching, morning dread, or exhaustion despite outward achievement. In other words, the nervous system has forgotten how to stop striving.

At the existential layer, perfectionism often reflects a deeper misunderstanding of human worth. Modern culture reinforces this misunderstanding continuously. Produce more, achieve more, optimize more, and perform more. Modern culture also reinforces be better, do better, and never stop.

Eventually many individuals lose the ability to distinguish between who they are, and what they accomplish. Rest begins feeling irresponsible; stillness begins feeling threatening; and sleep begins feeling unproductive. However, human beings are not machines. They are living systems requiring rhythm, restoration, limitation, flexibility, and imperfection.

At the SWEET Institute, we often emphasize that perfectionism is not strength; rather, it is chronic fear disguised as control; and control has a biological cost. The nervous system cannot remain in continuous optimization mode without eventually collapsing into exhaustion.

Healing perfectionism therefore requires more than simply "lowering standards." It requires helping the nervous system experience safety independent of flawless performance. This is where compassion becomes transformative: the ability to remain human without collapsing into shame. This changes sleep profoundly.

The individual slowly learns, "I can rest without earning it." "I can stop without everything falling apart." "I can make mistakes and still remain worthy." "I do not need complete certainty to release control."

This process takes time. The nervous system changes through repeated experiences of safe imperfection; and small moments matter and they include leaving something unfinished, going to bed before everything is complete, allowing uncertainty, accepting limitation, and choosing restoration over endless optimization.

At first, these moments often feel deeply uncomfortable. The perfectionistic nervous system interprets slowing down as danger. However, over time, flexibility increases. the body softens, and the mind quiets. The nervous system begins learning that survival no longer depends on constant striving.

Throughout this book, we will continue exploring how perfectionism interacts with insomnia, hypervigilance, emotional regulation, identity, trauma, attachment, and nervous system functioning across all four layers of transformation, for deep sleep does not emerge from perfect control; rather, it emerges when the nervous system no longer believes it must earn safety through endless performance.

The Exhaustion Cycle

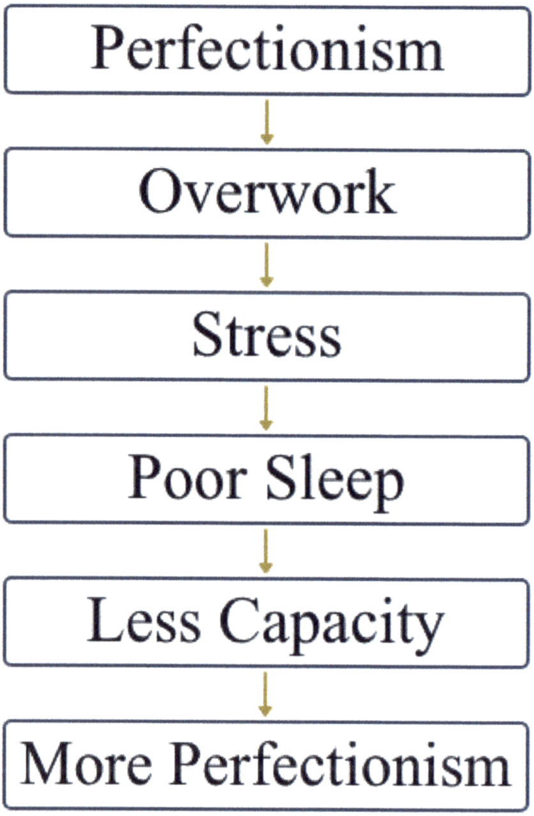

Selected Scientific References

- Burns, D. D. (1980). The perfectionist's script for self-defeat. *Psychology Today, 14*(6), 34–52.
- Perlis, M. L., Jungquist, C., Smith, M. T., & Posner, D. (2005). *Cognitive behavioral treatment of insomnia: A session-by-session guide*. Springer.
- Porges, S. W. (2011). *The polyvagal theory: Neurophysiological foundations of emotions, attachment, communication, and self-regulation*. W. W. Norton & Company.
- Shafran, R., Cooper, Z., & Fairburn, C. G. (2002). Clinical perfectionism: A cognitive-behavioural analysis. *Behaviour Research and Therapy, 40*(7), 773–791. https://doi.org/10.1016/S0005-7967(01)00059-6
- Siegel, D. J. (2012). *The developing mind: How relationships and the brain interact to shape who we are* (2nd ed.). Guilford Press.
- Van der Kolk, B. A. (2014). *The body keeps the score: Brain, mind, and body in the healing of trauma*. Viking.
- Walker, M. (2017). *Why we sleep: Unlocking the power of sleep and dreams*. Scribner.
- Young, J. E., Klosko, J. S., & Weishaar, M. E. (2003). *Schema therapy: A practitioner's guide*. Guilford Press.

Chapter 16 — Attachment, Loneliness, and the Night

At 2:23 a.m., Michael stared at the empty side of the bed again. The room was quiet, and perhaps too quiet. During the day, he could distract himself with work, meetings, messages, noise, movement, and responsibilities. However, nighttime was different. Nighttime removed distraction, and in the silence, loneliness became louder.

At the SWEET Institute, we recognize that sleep is not merely biological. Sleep is relational, and human nervous systems evolved in connection. For thousands of years, human beings slept near others: family, community, tribe, caregivers, and partners. Safety was collective.

The nervous system learned regulation through connection. This is why attachment profoundly affects sleep. The body does not simply ask, “Am I tired?” The body also asks, “Am I safe?” “Am I alone?” “Will anyone come if I need help?”

At the relational domain of the SWEET Multi-Domain Model, attachment experiences shape emotional regulation, autonomic functioning, stress recovery, nervous system development, trust, vulnerability, and the body’s capacity to release vigilance.

Secure attachment helps the nervous system learn, “I can relax.” “I am supported.” “I am not alone.” “The world is survivable.” Insecure attachment often teaches something different, “I must stay alert.” “I cannot depend on others.” “Connection is unpredictable.” “I must manage everything myself.” These relational templates frequently continue shaping sleep long into adulthood.

Research consistently demonstrates strong relationships between attachment insecurity, loneliness, emotional dysregulation, anxiety, hypervigilance, depression, and sleep disturbance. Chronic loneliness itself increases physiological stress activation, inflammatory processes, and sympathetic nervous system arousal while reducing restorative recovery. The nervous system experiences chronic disconnection as threat, as once again, human beings are relational organisms.

At the conscious layer of transformation, many individuals recognize practical nighttime patterns associated with loneliness and attachment distress: late-night texting, fear of silence, difficulty sleeping alone, constant checking behaviors, relationship rumination, or compulsive attempts to remain connected digitally. Others avoid emotional intimacy entirely and rely on distraction or hyper-independence instead. Both patterns often reflect attempts to manage relational fear.

At the psychological domain, nighttime frequently amplifies attachment anxiety because stillness reduces external distraction. Questions surface, "Am I loved?" "Am I abandoned?" "Am I enough?" "Will I always be alone?" The nervous system becomes activated not only by present reality, but by emotional memory.

At the pre-conscious layer, many individuals carry attachment schemas formed early in life. A child repeatedly left emotionally unseen may internalize, "I must handle everything alone." A child exposed to inconsistency may internalize, "Connection can disappear at any moment." A child criticized for emotional needs may internalize, "My vulnerability is dangerous." These beliefs shape adult nervous system functioning profoundly.

Some individuals become anxiously attached; hyper-alert to rejection, constantly monitoring connection, struggling to settle emotionally. Others become avoidantly attached; emotionally distant, hyper-independent, uncomfortable with vulnerability, and disconnected from emotional needs entirely.

Both patterns affect sleep. The anxiously attached nervous system struggles to release fear of abandonment. The avoidantly attached nervous system struggles to relax into emotional safety. The body remains vigilant in different ways.

At the unconscious layer, nighttime often reactivates unresolved relational wounds. Loneliness is rarely just the absence of people. Loneliness is often the absence of emotional safety. A person may be physically surrounded by others while remaining profoundly alone internally.

The unconscious mind remembers emotional neglect, betrayal, abandonment, rejection,

loss, or inconsistent caregiving. At night, when stimulation decreases, these emotional imprints may surface more intensely. The nervous system begins scanning for connection and protection.

Some individuals attempt to regulate this pain through scrolling, compulsive communication, food, substances, fantasy, or overthinking. Others shut down emotionally altogether. However, the body continues carrying the attachment burden.

At the existential layer, loneliness confronts human beings with some of life's deepest questions, "Am I truly seen?" "Am I lovable?" "Do I matter?" "Can I belong without performing?"

Modern society often intensifies disconnection despite constant digital contact. People communicate constantly yet feel emotionally unseen. The nervous system receives stimulation without nourishment. Information without intimacy, visibility without vulnerability, connection without safety, and exhausted nervous systems continue searching for regulation.

At the SWEET Institute, we often emphasize that healing sleep sometimes requires healing relationships, and not only with others, but with the self. This includes self-compassion, emotional honesty, safe connection, and boundary development. This also includes attachment repair, therapy, community, mindfulness, and learning how to remain emotionally present without collapsing into fear.

The nervous system slowly relearns, “I do not have to survive everything alone.” This changes sleep profoundly, for one of the deepest functions of attachment is shared regulation. A calm nervous system helps calm another nervous system, and this is why loving relationships often help people sleep more deeply.

The body feels safer, but equally important, individuals can gradually learn internal forms of regulation that help create safety even in solitude. This does not eliminate the human need for connection, but it strengthens the capacity to remain grounded without panic when alone. The nervous system becomes more flexible, less reactive, and more trusting.

Throughout this book, we will continue exploring how attachment, loneliness, trauma, regulation, environment, meaning, and nervous system functioning interact across all four layers of transformation. Deep sleep is not simply biological shutdown; rather, it often emerges when the nervous system no longer experiences aloneness as danger. It emerges when the body begins believing, “I am safe enough to let go.”

Attachment Styles and Nighttime Experience

Attachment Style	Core Belief	Typical Nighttime Experience	Common Sleep Difficulties
 **Secure**	*I am safe.* *Others are available.* *I can cope.*	**Calm body • Emotional safety • Ease with stillness • Self-soothing • Trust in tomorrow** Can settle relatively easily. Able to self-soothe. Nighttime feels restorative rather than threatening.	Occasional sleep disruption during periods of stress, but generally recovers quickly.
 **Anxious /Preoccupied**	*What if I'm abandoned?* *What if something goes wrong?*	**Racing thoughts • Checking phone • Replaying conversations • Catastrophizing • Needing reassurance • Separation distress** Mind becomes busy at night. Rumination increases. Worries about relationships, rejection, and future uncertainty. Strong need for reassurance.	Difficulty falling asleep, frequent awakenings, early morning anxiety.
 **Avoidant /Dismissive**	*I must rely on myself.* *Needs are dangerous or weak.*	**Avoids stillness • Keeps TV on • Doom scrolling • Suppresses feelings • Disconnects from body • Emotional numbing** May appear calm externally but remains physiologically activated. Difficulty softening into vulnerability. Uses work, television, scrolling, or distraction to avoid emotional contact.	Delayed sleep onset, late-night overstimulation, unrefreshing sleep.
 **Disorganized /Fearful**	*I want closeness, but closeness feels dangerous.*	**Hypervigilance • Nightmares • Panic • Intrusive memories • Loneliness and fear • Longing for safety • Startle response** Night may trigger fear, loneliness, hypervigilance, intrusive memories, or trauma activation. Simultaneous longing for comfort and fear of vulnerability.	Severe insomnia, nightmares, fragmented sleep, panic awakenings.

Healing Goals Across Attachment Styles

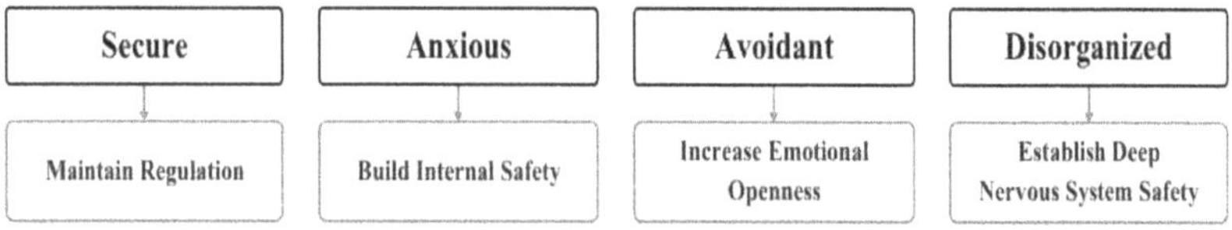

Selected Scientific References

- Bowlby, J. (1988). *A secure base: Parent-child attachment and healthy human development*. Basic Books.
- Cacioppo, J. T., & Patrick, W. (2008). *Loneliness: Human nature and the need for social connection*. W. W. Norton & Company.
- Johnson, S. M. (2019). *Attachment theory in practice: Emotionally focused therapy (EFT) with individuals, couples, and families*. Guilford Press.
- Perlis, M. L., Jungquist, C., Smith, M. T., & Posner, D. (2005). *Cognitive behavioral treatment of insomnia: A session-by-session guide*. Springer.
- Porges, S. W. (2011). *The polyvagal theory: Neurophysiological foundations of emotions, attachment, communication, and self-regulation*. W. W. Norton & Company.
- Siegel, D. J. (2012). *The developing mind: How relationships and the brain interact to shape who we are* (2nd ed.). Guilford Press.
- Van der Kolk, B. A. (2014). *The body keeps the score: Brain, mind, and body in the healing of trauma*. Viking.
- Walker, M. (2017). *Why we sleep: Unlocking the power of sleep and dreams*. Scribner.

Chapter 17 — Core Beliefs and Emotional Conditioning

At 1:48 a.m., Sofia's body was exhausted, but her mind remained alert. There was nothing dangerous happening, but something dangerous was expected.

She did not consciously think, "The world is unsafe," yet her nervous system behaved as though danger could appear at any moment.

Every sound startled her. Every uncertainty activated her. Every unfinished task felt threatening; and underneath it all lived a belief she had carried for years without fully realizing it, "I can never fully relax."

At the SWEET Institute, we recognize that human beings do not merely respond to present reality. They respond to emotional conditioning accumulated across a lifetime.

Experiences become patterns, patterns become beliefs, beliefs become physiology, and physiology eventually shapes sleep.

At the psychological domain of the SWEET Multi-Domain Model, core beliefs profoundly influence nervous system regulation, emotional interpretation, stress activation, relationship patterns, self-worth, and the body's ability to transition into restoration.

Core beliefs are not simply intellectual ideas. They are emotional truths the nervous system has learned through repeated experience. Some individuals carry beliefs such as, "The world is dangerous." "I must always stay prepared." "I am not safe." "I am alone." "I am responsible for everything." "My needs are too much." "If I stop, everything will fall apart."

These beliefs often operate automatically beneath conscious awareness; and because the nervous system listens continuously to emotional meaning, the body begins organizing itself around these assumptions.

Research consistently demonstrates that chronic stress conditioning, adverse childhood experiences, trauma exposure, insecure attachment, and maladaptive schemas significantly contribute to hypervigilance, anxiety disorders, insomnia, emotional dysregulation, and chronic physiological activation.

The body learns expectation, and this is why many people struggle to sleep even in objectively safe environments. The nervous system may still be responding to older emotional realities.

At the conscious layer of transformation, individuals often recognize certain repetitive thought patterns: catastrophizing, self-criticism, fear of failure, anticipatory anxiety, or chronic over-responsibility. However, these thoughts are often surface expressions of deeper emotional conditioning.

For example, "I need to check everything again" may reflect a deeper belief, "If I make a mistake, something terrible will happen." "I can't stop thinking about tomorrow"

may reflect, "I must stay hyper-alert to remain safe."

The conscious mind experiences the symptom, and the deeper nervous system carries the conditioning.

At the pre-conscious layer, schemas begin shaping how individuals interpret themselves, others, and the world automatically. This process often begins early.

A child raised in emotional unpredictability may internalize, "Danger appears suddenly." A child criticized repeatedly may internalize, "I must perform perfectly to be accepted." A child emotionally neglected may internalize, "My needs are not important."

A child forced into premature responsibility may internalize, "I must always remain in control."

These emotional learnings become nervous system expectations. The body adapts around them, and adaptation becomes identity.

The individual may later describe themselves as, "an anxious person," "a light sleeper,"

"someone who overthinks," or "someone whose brain never stops."

However, often these are conditioned survival responses rather than fixed personality traits.

At the unconscious layer, emotional conditioning continues operating automatically long after conscious awareness moves forward. The nervous system remembers patterns even when the conscious mind forgets events. This is why individuals may react intensely without fully understanding why.

A simple uncertainty may activate disproportionate physiological arousal because the body associates uncertainty with earlier emotional pain. Nighttime intensifies this process. Distraction decreases. Stillness increases. Awareness expands. And unresolved emotional conditioning becomes more noticeable.

The nervous system begins replaying old survival strategies: overthinking, preparing, monitoring, controlling, anticipating. The body attempts protection, but protection without release eventually becomes exhaustion.

At the existential layer, many individuals unknowingly organize entire lives around conditioned fear rather than conscious choice. They remain constantly vigilant, constantly productive, constantly prepared, and constantly emotionally guarded.

The nervous system never fully experiences permission to rest, but healing requires recognizing an important truth: Conditioning is powerful, but conditioning is not destiny, and the nervous system can relearn safety, though this process takes repetition.

At the SWEET Institute, we often emphasize that emotional conditioning changes through repeated corrective experiences across all domains of life. For example:

- Learning that mistakes do not destroy worth, learning that uncertainty can be tolerated,
- Learning that stillness is survivable, learning that vulnerability does not automatically create abandonment, and
- Learning that the body can soften without danger immediately following.

These experiences slowly reshape nervous system expectation; the body begins updating its predictions; and prediction shapes physiology.

This is why therapeutic work becomes so important for many individuals struggling with chronic insomnia and hypervigilance. Sleep problems are often not simply about nighttime. They are about lifelong conditioning. This may involve schema therapy, mindfulness, attachment repair, and trauma work. This may also involve cognitive restructuring, body-based regulation, self-compassion, free association, journaling, or emotionally corrective relationships.

The goal is not becoming perfectly calm. The goal is increasing flexibility. The nervous system slowly learns, "Not every uncertainty is danger." "Not every feeling requires escape." "Not every mistake threatens survival." Over time, the body softens. The mind slows. The nervous system releases chronic preparation, and sleep begins emerging more naturally.

Throughout this book, we will continue exploring how emotional conditioning interacts with sleep, identity, attachment, trauma, regulation, and meaning across all four layers of transformation, for deep sleep is not merely biological shutdown. It often begins when the nervous system stops expecting danger from life itself.

The Pre-Conscious Layer

Schema Map

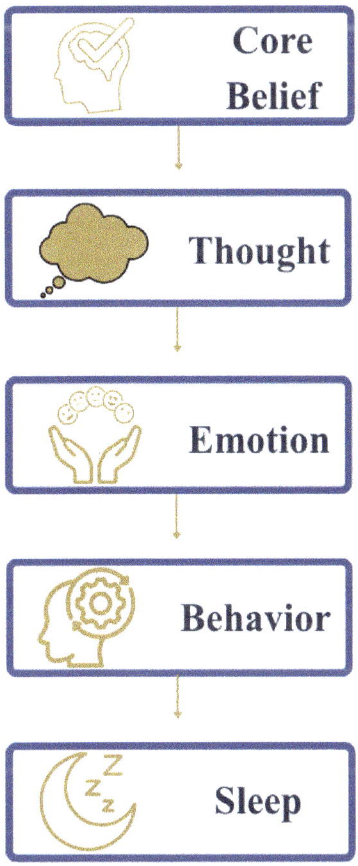

Selected Scientific References

- Beck, A. T. (1976). *Cognitive therapy and the emotional disorders*. International Universities Press.
- Linehan, M. M. (2015). *DBT skills training manual* (2nd ed.). Guilford Press.
- Perlis, M. L., Jungquist, C., Smith, M. T., & Posner, D. (2005). *Cognitive behavioral treatment of insomnia: A session-by-session guide*. Springer.
- Porges, S. W. (2011). *The polyvagal theory: Neurophysiological foundations of emotions, attachment, communication, and self-regulation*. W. W. Norton & Company.
- Siegel, D. J. (2012). *The developing mind: How relationships and the brain interact to shape who we are* (2nd ed.). Guilford Press.
- Van der Kolk, B. A. (2014). *The body keeps the score: Brain, mind, and body in the healing of trauma*. Viking.
- Walker, M. (2017). *Why we sleep: Unlocking the power of sleep and dreams*. Scribner.
- Young, J. E., Klosko, J. S., & Weishaar, M. E. (2003). *Schema therapy: A practitioner's guide*. Guilford Press.

Chapter 18 — Acceptance, Surrender, and Cognitive Defusion

At 2:41 a.m., Elena checked the clock again. Panic rose immediately. “If I don’t fall asleep now, tomorrow will be ruined.” Her body tightened, her breathing shortened, her mind accelerated, and the harder she tried to force sleep, the further sleep seemed to move away.

This is one of the great paradoxes of insomnia is that the more desperately people attempt to control sleep, the more activated the nervous system often becomes.

At the SWEET Institute, we recognize that sleep cannot be forced. Sleep emerges, and emergence requires conditions that support release rather than control.

This is where acceptance, surrender, and cognitive defusion become transformative, for chronic resistance itself often keeps the nervous system activated.

At the psychological domain of the SWEET Multi-Domain Model, many individuals struggling with insomnia become trapped not only by sleeplessness itself, but by their relationship to sleeplessness, characterized by ear of not sleeping, fear of tomorrow, fear of exhaustion, fear of losing control, and fear of failing again.

The nervous system begins treating wakefulness itself as danger, and once this cycle begins, bedtime becomes emotionally charged. The bed transforms from a place of restoration into a place of performance pressure. Research consistently demonstrates that sleep-related anxiety, catastrophic thinking, hyperarousal, and cognitive fusion significantly contribute to chronic insomnia. Efforts to force sleep frequently increase sympathetic activation, while acceptance-based approaches often reduce physiological arousal and improve sleep outcomes over time. The nervous system responds differently to pressure than to permission.

At the conscious layer of transformation, many individuals unknowingly intensify insomnia through internal struggle. Thoughts appear, "I have to sleep." "This is terrible." "I can't function tomorrow." "What's wrong with me?"

The mind begins fighting reality, and fighting activates the nervous system. This is why cognitive defusion becomes essential. Cognitive defusion, an important concept in Acceptance and Commitment Therapy (ACT), helps individuals recognize that thoughts are experiences occurring within consciousness rather than absolute truths requiring immediate belief or reaction.

A thought such as, "I'll never sleep." can be noticed as, "I am having the thought that I'll never sleep." This small shift creates psychological space. The individual stops fusing completely with the thought; and the nervous system experiences less threat. This does not magically eliminate insomnia, but it changes the relationship to insomnia, and relationship changes physiology.

At the pre-conscious layer, many individuals carry deeply conditioned beliefs about control. "If I relax, something bad will happen." "If I am not constantly prepared, I will fail." "I must control every outcome." These schemas often develop in environments where unpredictability felt dangerous.

The nervous system adapted by increasing monitoring and control, but sleep requires the opposite movement. Sleep requires surrender, yet for many individuals, surrender feels terrifying, for the nervous system associates release with vulnerability.

At the unconscious layer, insomnia itself may become emotionally loaded. Some individuals unconsciously fear dreams. Some fear stillness. Some fear emotional contact. Some fear the loss of control associated with sleep itself.

The unconscious mind often attempts protection through vigilance. The body stays awake because wakefulness feels safer than release. This is why aggressive attempts to "defeat insomnia" frequently fail. The nervous system interprets the battle itself as further danger, yet healing often begins not when the person forces sleep harder, but when the nervous system no longer experiences wakefulness as catastrophic.

At the existential layer, acceptance becomes deeply misunderstood in modern culture. People often confuse acceptance with resignation, yet acceptance is not surrendering hope; rather, acceptance is surrendering unnecessary war with reality.

There is enormous difference between, "I give up," and "I stop fighting this moment." The nervous system softens when resistance decreases.

At the SWEET Institute, we often emphasize that healing requires learning how to coexist temporarily with discomfort without immediately collapsing into panic or avoidance. This applies profoundly to sleep. A person lying awake may initially experience fear, frustration, anger, helplessness, or catastrophic thinking.

However, if the individual learns to respond with breath awareness, gentle observation, self-compassion, and reduced struggle, the nervous system often gradually downregulates. The body begins receiving a new message, "Wakefulness is uncomfortable, but it is not an emergency."

This shift is powerful for the nervous system no longer escalates automatically into survival mode, and one of the most important paradoxes in sleep healing is this: People often sleep better when they stop trying so desperately to force sleep, for otherwise desperate control frequently signals danger to the nervous system.

Sleep emerges more naturally when pressure decreases. This is why many individuals unexpectedly fall asleep: while reading calmly, during quiet relaxation, after releasing obsessive monitoring, or once they emotionally stop fighting the experience itself. The nervous system responds to emotional tone.

At the SWEET Institute, we often encourage individuals to practice compassionate surrender at night. "I can allow this moment without attacking myself," instead of "I must sleep immediately." "My nervous system is activated, and activation changes," instead of "I am broken." "I can tolerate uncertainty safely," instead of "I need total control."

This process builds emotional flexibility. The body learns, "We do not have to panic every time discomfort appears," and emotional flexibility profoundly supports restoration.

Throughout this book, we will continue exploring how acceptance, mindfulness, emotional regulation, unconscious integration, and existential surrender interact across all four layers of transformation, for deep sleep is not created through force. It often emerges the moment the nervous system no longer believes it must stay awake to maintain control. It emerges when the body finally understands, "It is safe to let go."

Selected Scientific References

- Beck, A. T. (1976). *Cognitive therapy and the emotional disorders*. International Universities Press.
- Hayes, S. C., Strosahl, K. D., & Wilson, K. G. (2016). *Acceptance and commitment therapy: The process and practice of mindful change* (2nd ed.). Guilford Press.
- Kabat-Zinn, J. (1990). *Full catastrophe living: Using the wisdom of your body and mind to face stress, pain, and illness*. Dell Publishing.
- Perlis, M. L., Jungquist, C., Smith, M. T., & Posner, D. (2005). *Cognitive behavioral treatment of insomnia: A session-by-session guide*. Springer.
- Porges, S. W. (2011). *The polyvagal theory: Neurophysiological foundations of emotions, attachment, communication, and self-regulation*. W. W. Norton & Company.
- Siegel, D. J. (2012). *The developing mind: How relationships and the brain interact to shape who we are* (2nd ed.). Guilford Press.
- Van der Kolk, B. A. (2014). *The body keeps the score: Brain, mind, and body in the healing of trauma*. Viking.
- Walker, M. (2017). *Why we sleep: Unlocking the power of sleep and dreams*. Scribner.

Chapter 19 — Learning Psychological Safety

At 3:02 a.m., Vanessa sat awake in the dark again. There was no emergency, no crisis, no immediate threat; yet her body remained tense. Her jaw clenched, her shoulders tightened, her thoughts raced, and her nervous system stayed alert as though something terrible might happen at any moment. Without realizing it, she had spent most of her life surviving instead of feeling safe.

At the SWEET Institute, we recognize that psychological safety is one of the most misunderstood dimensions of healing. Many people assume safety means the absence of external danger. However, psychological safety is deeper than circumstance.

Psychological safety is the nervous system's internal experience of permission,

trust, predictability, emotional security, and the belief that one can exist without constant preparation for harm.

A person may live in an objectively safe environment while remaining internally terrified. The body continues responding to older emotional realities, and this profoundly affects sleep. Sleep requires vulnerability, sleep requires release, and sleep requires the nervous system to temporarily stop scanning. However, many individuals never fully learned how to do that.

At the relational and psychological domains of the SWEET Multi-Domain Model, psychological safety develops through repeated experiences of attunement, consistency, emotional responsiveness, protection, and trustworthy connection.

Children whose emotional needs are repeatedly met often internalize, “I am safe enough to relax.” Children raised in chronic unpredictability, criticism, instability, neglect, conflict, trauma, or emotional inconsistency often internalize something different, “I must stay prepared.” The nervous system adapts around these experiences, and adaptation becomes physiology. Research consistently demonstrates that chronic stress exposure, trauma histories, insecure attachment, adverse childhood experiences, and prolonged emotional unpredictability significantly impact autonomic regulation, emotional processing, sleep quality, hypervigilance, and long-term nervous system functioning.

The body learns expectation, and expectation shapes biology. This is why many individuals struggling with insomnia are not simply “thinking too much.” Their nervous systems never fully exit survival mode.

At the conscious layer of transformation, many people attempt to improve sleep through behavioral changes alone: better routines, less caffeine, improved sleep hygiene, and reduced stimulation. These interventions matter tremendously, but behavioral interventions often fail when the nervous system still perceives rest itself as unsafe.

This creates a painful paradox. The exhausted individual desperately wants sleep, yet the nervous system simultaneously resists surrender.

At the psychological domain, individuals frequently experience automatic thoughts such as, “I can’t relax.” “I have to stay alert.” “Something bad will happen.” “I can’t let my guard down.” These thoughts are not random. They reflect conditioned survival patterns.

At the pre-conscious layer, many individuals carry emotional schemas organized around danger, unpredictability, abandonment, shame, or hyper-responsibility.

The nervous system learned safety is temporary, vulnerability is risky, stillness is dangerous, or emotional needs create disappointment. These beliefs often continue shaping physiology long after conscious awareness recognizes they are no longer entirely true. The body still remembers.

At the unconscious layer, psychological unsafety frequently persists through implicit emotional memory. Some individuals unconsciously fear silence because silence previously preceded conflict.

Some fear nighttime because nighttime was associated with loneliness, unpredictability, or trauma. Some fear vulnerability because dependence once resulted in emotional pain.

The unconscious mind continuously attempts protection through vigilance. The body stays prepared, and preparation prevents deep restoration. This is why healing sleep often requires more than symptom reduction. It requires helping the nervous system experience corrective emotional reality.

At the existential layer, psychological safety also involves a deeper relationship with life itself. Many individuals unconsciously experience existence as fundamentally unsafe, always waiting, always preparing, always bracing, and always anticipating loss, failure, criticism, abandonment, or catastrophe. The nervous system remains exhausted because it never fully trusts life enough to soften. However, healing gradually introduces a different possibility: Safety is not the absence of uncertainty. Safcty is thc growing ability to remain grounded even in the presence of uncertainty.

This distinction changes everything, for life will always contain unpredictability, but the nervous system no longer has to interpret every uncertainty as immediate danger.

At the SWEET Institute, we often emphasize that psychological safety develops through repeated regulating experiences. Once again, small moments matter. They include being listened to without judgment, resting without punishment, expressing emotion safely, and experiencing consistency. They also include setting boundaries, receiving compassion, slowing down without catastrophe following, allowing imperfection, and discovering that vulnerability can coexist with safety.

These experiences slowly reshape nervous system expectation. The body begins updating its predictions, and prediction shapes sleep profoundly. The nervous system slowly learns, "We no longer have to remain on guard every moment." Once again, his process takes time, especially for individuals whose nervous systems adapted around chronic vigilance.

Healing often feels unfamiliar at first. Some individuals initially become more anxious when slowing down because activation itself became normal. Stillness may initially feel unsafe. However, with repetition, the body gradually learns another possibility; calm without collapse, rest without danger, and silence without catastrophe.

This is where compassion becomes essential. The goal is not forcing the nervous system into relaxation. The goal is creating conditions where the body gradually trusts release.

Throughout this book, we will continue exploring how psychological safety develops across Biological, Psychological, Relational, Environmental, and Existential domains simultaneously, for deep sleep is not simply about physical exhaustion. Rather, it often emerges when the nervous system no longer experiences existence itself as an emergency. Deep sleep emerges when the body finally learns, "We survived." "And now, we are allowed to rest."

Selected Scientific References

- Bowlby, J. (1988). *A secure base: Parent-child attachment and healthy human development*. Basic Books.
- Cozolino, L. (2014). *The neuroscience of human relationships: Attachment and the developing social brain* (2nd ed.). W. W. Norton & Company.
- Johnson, S. M. (2019). *Attachment theory in practice: Emotionally focused therapy (EFT) with individuals, couples, and families*. Guilford Press.
- Perlis, M. L., Jungquist, C., Smith, M. T., & Posner, D. (2005). *Cognitive behavioral treatment of insomnia: A session-by-session guide*. Springer.
- Porges, S. W. (2011). *The polyvagal theory: Neurophysiological foundations of emotions, attachment, communication, and self-regulation*. W. W. Norton & Company.
- Siegel, D. J. (2012). *The developing mind: How relationships and the brain interact to shape who we are* (2nd ed.). Guilford Press.
- Van der Kolk, B. A. (2014). *The body keeps the score: Brain, mind, and body in the healing of trauma*. Viking.
- Walker, M. (2017). *Why we sleep: Unlocking the power of sleep and dreams*. Scribner.

Part IV – The Unconscious Layer

Chapter 20 — Dreams as Communication

At 4:11 a.m., Amelia woke suddenly from another vivid dream. Her heart was racing, and the images lingered: a hallway, a locked door, a child crying, water rising, and someone disappearing before she could reach them.

She sat in silence trying to understand why the dream felt more emotionally real than most moments of her waking day.

By morning, she dismissed it. "Just a dream," she told herself. However, part of her knew it was more than that.

At the SWEET Institute, we recognize that dreams are not random mental garbage. Dreams are communication. The unconscious mind speaks symbolically; and nighttime often becomes one of the few spaces where deeply buried emotional material can emerge without the defenses and distractions that dominate waking life.

Human beings do not stop processing emotionally during sleep. In many ways, emotional processing intensifies.

At the unconscious domain of the SWEET Multi-Domain Model, dreams frequently reflect unresolved conflicts, emotional memories, fears, wishes, grief, attachment dynamics, internal tensions, symbolic narratives, and nervous system attempts at integration.

The dreaming mind speaks in metaphor. A collapsing house may symbolize psychological instability; being chased may symbolize unresolved fear or avoidance; losing one's voice may symbolize emotional suppression; missing a train may symbolize anxiety about time, failure, opportunity, or loss.

Dreams rarely communicate literally. They communicate emotionally. Research increasingly demonstrates that REM sleep plays an important role in emotional processing, memory integration, fear modulation, learning, and nervous system recovery. Dream activity appears closely linked with emotional regulation and the integration of waking experiences into broader psychological meaning systems. The sleeping mind continues working.

At the biological domain, REM sleep significantly supports emotional memory processing and nervous system recalibration. Chronic sleep disruption often interferes with emotional integration itself.

This is one reason emotionally distressed individuals frequently experience vivid dreams, nightmares, fragmented sleep, or emotionally intense nighttime activation. The nervous system attempts processing even when conscious awareness avoids it.

At the conscious layer of transformation, many people ignore dreams entirely because modern culture often dismisses symbolic inner experience. However, throughout human history, dreams have carried enormous psychological, spiritual, relational, and existential significance.

At the SWEET Institute, we encourage individuals not to treat dreams as magical predictions, but as meaningful psychological communication.

The question is not, "Is this dream literally true?" The deeper question is, "What emotional truth might this dream be expressing?"

Dreams often reveal emotional realities the waking mind minimizes, including fear, longing, grief, shame, conflict, desire, unresolved pain, unspoken truth.

At the psychological domain, dreams may also reflect unresolved daytime emotional activation. A person suppressing anger consciously may dream of explosions. A person terrified of abandonment may dream repeatedly of losing loved ones. A perfectionistic individual may dream of failure, chaos, or exposure.

The unconscious mind organizes emotional material symbolically because direct contact may initially feel overwhelming.

At the pre-conscious layer, repeated dream themes often reveal underlying schemas. Dreams may reflect deeper emotional conditioning shaped through earlier relational experiences. They may involve being trapped, being chased, being invisible, and being criticized. They may also involve being abandoned, or being unprepared

The nervous system continues replaying unresolved emotional patterns until integration begins occurring consciously. This is why recurring dreams are often psychologically important. The mind keeps repeating the emotional message because something remains unfinished.

At the unconscious layer, dreams sometimes bypass defenses entirely. During waking life, individuals often distract, suppress, intellectualize, avoid, or overwork to escape emotional contact. However, sleep softens many defenses. Symbolic material emerges, and the unconscious speaks.

This does not mean every dream requires intense analysis. However, it does mean dreams deserve curiosity rather than dismissal.

At the existential layer, dreams reconnect human beings with mystery. Modern society often overvalues only what can be measured externally, but human beings are not purely rational systems. They are symbolic beings, emotional beings, narrative beings, and meaning-making beings.

Dreams remind us that life exists not only on the surface of consciousness. There are deeper layers continuously shaping experience. This is one reason dream reflection can become profoundly healing, for dreams reconnect individuals with parts of themselves long ignored.

At the SWEET Institute, we often encourage gentle dream exploration practices such as dream journaling, free association, reflective inquiry, mindfulness, and emotional curiosity.

Simple questions matter, “What emotions were present?” “What in my waking life feels emotionally similar?” “What might this symbolize?” “What unresolved experience could this reflect?”

The goal is not rigid interpretation. The goal is relationship, including relationship with the unconscious, relationship with emotional truth, and relationship with self. This becomes especially important for individuals whose lives are dominated by chronic external stimulation.

Dreams slow people down. They invite listening, integration, and often, their emotional intensity reveals how much unresolved material the nervous system has been carrying silently.

Nightmares themselves are important communication. A nightmare is often not the nervous system trying to punish someone. It is frequently the nervous system attempting to process overwhelming emotional material that has not yet been fully integrated. The body continues trying to metabolize emotional experience and healing requires compassion rather than fear toward these processes.

Throughout this book, we will continue exploring how dreams interact with trauma, attachment, emotional regulation, unconscious conflict, identity, and existential meaning across all four layers of transformation, for deep sleep is not simply unconsciousness. It is also a doorway into the deeper emotional life continuously unfolding beneath conscious awareness. Sometimes, while the body sleeps, the unconscious mind quietly continues trying to help us heal.

Dreams

Dreams as Messages

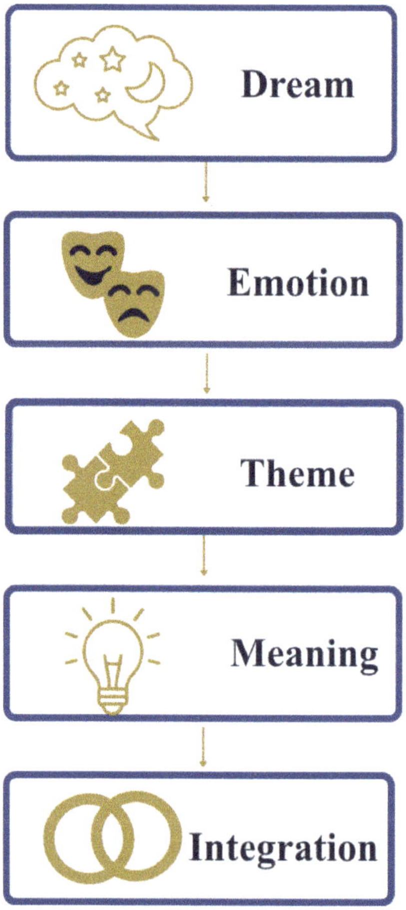

Selected Scientific References

- Freud, S. (1900/2010). *The interpretation of dreams*. Basic Books.
- *(If you used a different edition or publisher, substitute the appropriate publication year and publisher.)*
- Hartmann, E. (1998). *Dreams and nightmares: The origin and meaning of dreams*. Plenum Trade.
- Jung, C. G. (1964). *Man and his symbols*. Dell Publishing.
- Perlis, M. L., Jungquist, C., Smith, M. T., & Posner, D. (2005). *Cognitive behavioral treatment of insomnia: A session-by-session guide*. Springer.
- Porges, S. W. (2011). *The polyvagal theory: Neurophysiological foundations of emotions, attachment, communication, and self-regulation*. W. W. Norton & Company.
- Siegel, D. J. (2012). *The developing mind: How relationships and the brain interact to shape who we are* (2nd ed.). Guilford Press.
- Van der Kolk, B. A. (2014). *The body keeps the score: Brain, mind, and body in the healing of trauma*. Viking.
- Walker, M. (2017). *Why we sleep: Unlocking the power of sleep and dreams*. Scribner.

Chapter 21 — The Repressed Emotional Life

At 3:17 a.m., Marcus woke up suddenly with a crushing heaviness in his chest. There was no obvious thought that triggered it, and there was no immediate danger existed. Yet his body felt flooded with emotion he could not explain. He sat in silence trying to push the feeling away, but the harder he resisted, the stronger it became.

At the SWEET Institute, we recognize that the human mind does not simply forget painful emotional experiences. Many emotions become suppressed, avoided, disconnected from awareness, intellectualized, or buried beneath layers of survival adaptation. Yet what is repressed psychologically often continues existing physiologically.

The body remembers, and nighttime frequently becomes one of the few moments when the unconscious mind begins surfacing what waking life continuously suppresses.

At the unconscious domain of the SWEET Multi-Domain Model, unresolved emotional experiences continue shaping nervous system activation, stress responses, dreams, sleep quality, emotional regulation, bodily tension, and psychological functioning long after conscious awareness attempts to move forward.

Human beings are not designed merely to experience emotion. They are designed to process emotion. When emotional experiences remain unprocessed, the nervous system continues carrying them. Grief remains in the body, ear remains in the body, shame remains in the body, rage remains in the body, and loneliness remains in the body.

Often, the body continues communicating what the conscious mind has stopped listening to. Research increasingly demonstrates that trauma exposure, emotional suppression, chronic stress, unresolved grief, and adverse emotional experiences significantly affect autonomic regulation, inflammatory processes, sleep architecture, emotional processing, and nervous system recovery.

The unconscious mind continues influencing physiology continuously. This is one reason individuals sometimes experience nightmares, panic awakenings, muscular tension, and chronic hypervigilance. This is why they also experience emotional numbness, sleep fragmentation, or unexplained nighttime anxiety. The body continues carrying emotional burden beneath conscious awareness.

At the conscious layer of transformation, many individuals are highly skilled at avoidance. They remain busy constantly, they overwork, they distract, they scroll, and they intellectualize. They also stay productive, and they consume stimulation continuously because stillness threatens emotional contact.

Nighttime changes this dynamic. Distraction decreases. Silence increases, and emotional material long suppressed may begin surfacing into awareness. This is one reason many people become emotionally overwhelmed at night without fully understanding why. The unconscious mind is less distracted.

At the psychological domain, emotional suppression often initially appears adaptive. A child growing up in instability may learn, "Do not cry." Another may learn, "Your needs overwhelm people." Another, "Vulnerability is dangerous." The nervous system adapts through emotional constriction, and over time, suppression becomes automatic.

The individual disconnects from emotional awareness itself, but disconnection is not resolution, for the body still carries the emotional charge.

At the pre-conscious layer, unresolved emotional experiences often organize internal patterns without conscious recognition. A person carrying unresolved grief may become chronically restless. A person carrying suppressed anger may experience chronic tension. A person carrying shame may remain perpetually hypervigilant. A person carrying abandonment wounds may fear stillness because stillness reconnects them with loneliness. The nervous system continues organizing around unfinished emotional experience.

At the unconscious layer, the mind continuously attempts both protection and expression simultaneously. Defenses emerge, including intellectualization, avoidance, perfectionism, and overworking. They also include humor, substance use, control, distraction, or emotional numbing. These defenses are survival adaptations.

However, survival adaptations often become costly when they permanently disconnect individuals from emotional processing. The nervous system remains burdened by what has not been integrated. This is why healing requires more than symptom management.

Healing requires emotional contact, without overwhelming emotional flooding. It requires gradual, safe, compassionate contact with what has been carried silently.

At the existential layer, many individuals eventually realize they have spent years trying not to feel. In trying not to feel pain, they also lost access to portions of joy, aliveness, vulnerability, intimacy, creativity, and presence.

Emotional suppression narrows life. The nervous system becomes organized around avoidance rather than openness, and healing reintroduces another possibility: The body can survive emotion. This becomes revolutionary for many individuals, especially those whose nervous systems learned that emotional expression created danger, rejection, chaos, or abandonment.

At the SWEET Institute, we often emphasize that emotions themselves are not enemies.

Emotion is communication. Emotion is movement. Emotion is information. The problem is rarely emotion itself. The problem is unsupported emotional overwhelm. This is why safe processing matters, whether it is through therapy, journaling, mindfulness, or free association. Whether it is through dream exploration, body awareness, breath awareness, safe relationships, and reflective practices, the nervous system gradually increases its capacity to remain present with emotional experience without collapsing into panic or avoidance.

The body slowly learns, "We no longer need to suppress everything to survive." This changes sleep profoundly because the nervous system no longer has to remain chronically activated protecting against emotional contact. The body softens. The mind quiets, and the unconscious becomes less burdened by unfinished emotional material demanding expression. Healing then takes time, especially for individuals who spent years surviving through emotional disconnection.

However, the nervous system changes through repeated experiences of safe emotional integration, and often, the symptoms people fear most are actually attempts at communication from parts of the self that were never fully allowed to speak.

Throughout this book, we will continue exploring how repression, trauma, attachment, emotional integration, identity, meaning, and nervous system regulation interact across all four layers of transformation, for deep sleep is not simply the absence of wakefulness. Deep sleep often emerges when the nervous system no longer has to spend the entire night protecting the self from its own unprocessed emotional life.

The Unconscious Layer

The Iceberg Model

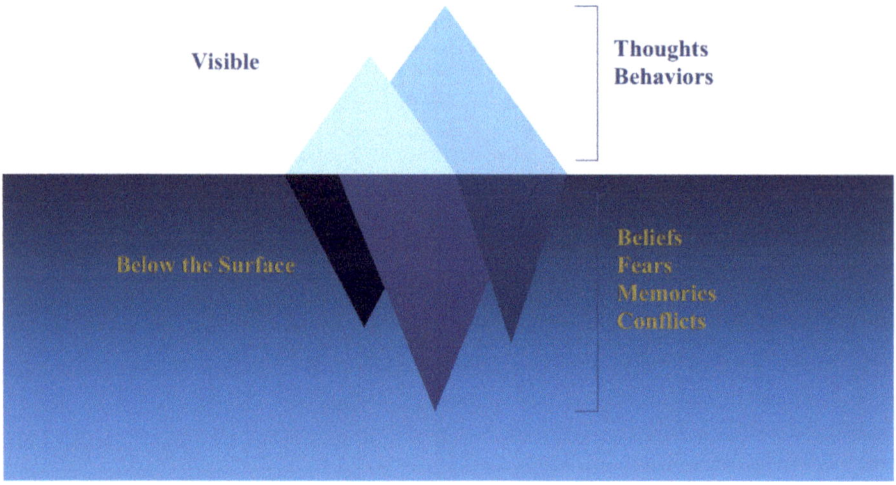

Selected Scientific References

- Freud, S. (1915/1957). Repression. In J. Strachey (Ed. & Trans.), *The standard edition of the complete psychological works of Sigmund Freud* (Vol. 14, pp. 141–158). Hogarth Press.
- *(If you used a different edition of Freud's works, substitute that publication information.)*
- Kabat-Zinn, J. (1990). *Full catastrophe living: Using the wisdom of your body and mind to face stress, pain, and illness*. Dell Publishing.
- Levine, P. A. (2010). *In an unspoken voice: How the body releases trauma and restores goodness*. North Atlantic Books.
- Perlis, M. L., Jungquist, C., Smith, M. T., & Posner, D. (2005). *Cognitive behavioral treatment of insomnia: A session-by-session guide*. Springer.
- Porges, S. W. (2011). *The polyvagal theory: Neurophysiological foundations of emotions, attachment, communication, and self-regulation*. W. W. Norton & Company.
- Siegel, D. J. (2012). *The developing mind: How relationships and the brain interact to shape who we are* (2nd ed.). Guilford Press.
- Van der Kolk, B. A. (2014). *The body keeps the score: Brain, mind, and body in the healing of trauma*. Viking.
- Walker, M. (2017). *Why we sleep: Unlocking the power of sleep and dreams*. Scribner.

Chapter 22 — Working Through: Rewiring the Sleeping Mind

At 1:56 a.m., Teresa noticed something different. For years, bedtime had triggered immediate anxiety: the same racing thoughts, the same tightness in her chest, and the same fear that sleep would never come.

However, tonight, although the thoughts still appeared, something had shifted. She no longer believed she was trapped inside them. Her body still carried old patterns, but her relationship to those patterns had begun changing, and that changed everything.

At the SWEET Institute, we recognize that healing is not merely insight. Healing is integration, and many individuals intellectually understand their struggles long before their nervous systems fully change. Someone may know, "My childhood was unpredictable." "I struggle with hypervigilance." "My perfectionism is fear-based." Yet despite this awareness, the body may continue reacting automatically. This is why working through becomes essential.

Working through refers to the repeated process of revisiting, understanding, emotionally processing, practicing, integrating, and gradually reshaping longstanding psychological and nervous system patterns over time. Healing occurs through repetition, and the nervous system changes slowly.

At the biological domain of the SWEET Multi-Domain Model, repeated experiences gradually reshape neural pathways, autonomic responses, emotional associations, and physiological regulation systems. The brain is plastic. The nervous system learns through repeated activation patterns. This means chronic fear strengthens fear pathways, but repeated safety experiences strengthen regulation pathways, and this is extraordinarily hopeful, for conditioned suffering is not permanent.

Research consistently demonstrates that neuroplasticity allows the nervous system to reorganize through repeated corrective experiences, mindfulness practices, emotional regulation work, relational safety, behavioral consistency, trauma processing, and cognitive restructuring. The body learns through experience. This is why people often become frustrated during healing. They expect insight to create immediate transformation. However, awareness is only the beginning. The nervous system requires repetition to update deeply conditioned expectations.

At the conscious layer of transformation, working through involves repeatedly practicing new behaviors even when old patterns still feel automatic. Going to bed earlier consistently; reducing stimulation; using breath awareness; and interrupting catastrophic thinking. Additional ones include allowing imperfection, creating rituals, choosing rest and practicing self-compassion.

These actions may initially feel unfamiliar or emotionally uncomfortable because the nervous system remains conditioned around older patterns. However, repetition creates new learning.

At the psychological domain, working through also means revisiting emotional themes repeatedly with increasing awareness and flexibility. For example, recognizing perfectionism when it appears, noticing attachment fears, observing catastrophic thinking, identifying emotional avoidance, or understanding how internal dialogue shapes physiology. The goal is not perfection; rather, the goal is growing awareness and flexibility over time.

At the pre-conscious layer, emotional schemas gradually soften through repeated corrective emotional experiences. A person who learned, "I am never safe," slowly begins experiencing moments of safety. A person who learned, "I must stay hyper-alert," begins discovering that stillness can be tolerated. A person who learned, "My worth depends on performance," begins practicing rest without earning it. These experiences gradually reshape nervous system expectation, and the body updates its predictions through lived experience.

At the unconscious layer, working through involves repeatedly allowing emotional material into awareness safely enough for integration to occur. This may include dream reflection, free association, journaling, and therapy. This may also include mindfulness, body awareness, emotional processing, or recognizing recurring relational patterns.

The unconscious mind often repeats unresolved material not to punish the individual, but because something unfinished continues seeking integration. This is why healing rarely happens in a perfectly linear way. Old fears may reappear, old dreams may return, and old anxieties may reactivate. This does not necessarily mean healing failed; rather, it often means deeper layers are emerging for integration.

At the existential layer, working through requires patience with human complexity. Modern culture often promises rapid transformation: quick fixes, instant optimization, and overnight solutions. However, human beings are layered. Healing takes time because the nervous system developed through years of experience. Integration unfolds gradually, and this becomes especially important around sleep healing.

Many individuals attack themselves when progress is imperfect, "I'm back to square one." "I should be over this." "Why am I still struggling?" However, nervous system healing rarely moves in straight lines. There are waves, fluctuations, periods of progress.

Periods of resurfacing. The goal is not perfection; rather, the goal is increasing regulation, flexibility, awareness, and self-compassion over time.

At the SWEET Institute, we often emphasize a central truth: What is repeated becomes strengthened. Repeated fear strengthens fear; repeated avoidance strengthens avoidance; and repeated safety strengthens safety. Further, repeated compassion strengthens compassion; and repeated regulation strengthens regulation.

This principle changes everything, for small actions matter enormously over time. One compassionate response instead of self-attack; one regulated pause instead of impulsive reaction; and one evening ritual; in addition to one moment of breath awareness, one boundary, and one experience of resting without guilt.

The nervous system learns through accumulation. This is why sustainable healing is built through consistency rather than intensity. People often search for dramatic transformation while overlooking the biological power of small, repeated experiences. However, small experiences repeated consistently reshape identity itself. The body softens, the mind quiets, and the nervous system becomes less reactive. Sleep gradually deepens, and the individual slowly begins trusting life differently, for the nervous system no longer organizes around constant survival.

Throughout this book, we have explored how sleep interacts with biology, emotion, attachment, trauma, internal dialogue, conditioning, meaning, and unconscious life across all four layers of transformation. An important realization emerges: Healing sleep is not merely about nighttime. Healing sleep reflects the gradual reorganization of the entire nervous system. Deep sleep emerges when the body no longer needs to remain chronically prepared for danger. It emerges when the nervous system learns through repeated lived experience that restoration is finally possible, and that learning happens one compassionate repetition at a time.

Working Through

Transformation Spiral

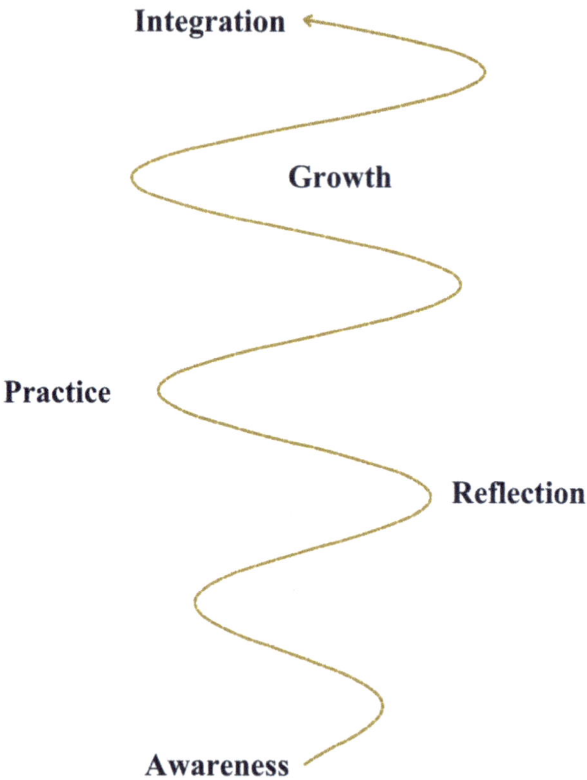

Selected Scientific References

- Hayes, S. C., Strosahl, K. D., & Wilson, K. G. (2016). *Acceptance and commitment therapy: The process and practice of mindful change* (2nd ed.). Guilford Press.
- Levine, P. A. (2010). *In an unspoken voice: How the body releases trauma and restores goodness*. North Atlantic Books.
- Linehan, M. M. (2015). *DBT skills training manual* (2nd ed.). Guilford Press.
- Perlis, M. L., Jungquist, C., Smith, M. T., & Posner, D. (2005). *Cognitive behavioral treatment of insomnia: A session-by-session guide*. Springer.
- Porges, S. W. (2011). *The polyvagal theory: Neurophysiological foundations of emotions, attachment, communication, and self-regulation*. W. W. Norton & Company.
- Siegel, D. J. (2012). *The developing mind: How relationships and the brain interact to shape who we are* (2nd ed.). Guilford Press.
- Van der Kolk, B. A. (2014). *The body keeps the score: Brain, mind, and body in the healing of trauma*. Viking.
- Walker, M. (2017). *Why we sleep: Unlocking the power of sleep and dreams*. Scribner.

Part V – The Existential Layer

Chapter 23 — Meaning, Purpose, and the Rested Life

At 5:38 a.m., Ethan sat quietly watching the sunrise after another difficult night, yet something felt different. For years, he had approached sleep like a battle: something to force, something to control, and something to conquer. Yet lately, another question had begun emerging inside him, “What kind of life is my nervous system trying to survive?” That question changed everything.

At the SWEET Institute, we recognize that healing sleep ultimately becomes larger than sleep itself, for exhaustion is not always caused only by lack of rest. Sometimes people are exhausted by the lives they are living. Sometimes they are exhausted by constant performance, disconnection, lack of meaning, and chronic urgency. Sometimes they are exhausted by unresolved grief, relational emptiness, misalignment, or endless striving disconnected from purpose.

The nervous system responds not only to behavior, but to meaning, and human beings are not merely biological organisms. They are existential beings, and when life loses meaning, the body often loses rhythm.

At the existential domain of the SWEET Multi-Domain Model, purpose, identity, values, belonging, spirituality, freedom, contribution, and meaning profoundly shape emotional regulation, resilience, nervous system functioning, and psychological vitality. This is why some individuals remain exhausted even after improving sleep hygiene. The body may be asking deeper questions.

Research consistently demonstrates strong associations between meaning, purpose, emotional well-being, resilience, stress regulation, mental health, and overall physiological functioning. Individuals with greater perceived meaning and connectedness often demonstrate improved emotional flexibility, lower chronic stress activation, and greater psychological resilience. Meaning affects biology, and this is profoundly important.

At the conscious layer of transformation, many individuals initially approach healing sleep behaviorally: better routines, less stimulation, consistent wake times, and improved regulation. These matter tremendously, but eventually another layer emerges:

"How am I living?" Am I constantly rushing? Am I living disconnected from my values? Am I carrying relationships that drain the nervous system continuously? Am I living only reactively? Am I allowing joy, play, connection, contribution, creativity, stillness, and meaning into my life? The body listens to these realities.

At the psychological domain, many individuals unconsciously organize their lives around survival rather than aliveness, always preparing, always producing, always reacting, and always proving. The nervous system never fully experiences restoration because the individual never fully experiences psychological arrival.

There is always another task: another goal, another fear, another emergency, and another performance. The body remains mobilized.

At the pre-conscious layer, many individuals carry schemas equating worth with productivity. "If I stop, I lose value." "If I rest, I am lazy." "If I am not achieving, I am failing." These beliefs create chronic internal pressure. Even moments of stillness become contaminated by guilt. The nervous system never fully relaxes because identity itself becomes attached to performance.

At the unconscious layer, chronic overworking and endless striving sometimes function defensively. Achievement may protect against shame. Busyness may protect against grief. Productivity may protect against emptiness; and success may protect against feelings of inadequacy. The unconscious mind often uses activity to avoid emotional vulnerability. However, eventually the nervous system becomes exhausted from endless compensation.

At the existential layer, healing requires a profound shift. Life cannot be only survival. Human beings require meaning, connection, beauty, and purpose. Human beings also require presence, play, love, creativity, and contribution. Without these experiences, the nervous system often remains spiritually depleted even when physically functioning. This is why some people feel exhausted despite "doing everything right," For the body may be longing not only for sleep, but for alignment.

At the SWEET Institute, we often emphasize that true restoration emerges when body, mind, and meaning begin moving together again. This is the essence of the SWEET Body–Mind–Meaning Framework. The body needs regulation; the mind needs flexibility; meaning systems need coherence; and when these dimensions become fragmented, the nervous system struggles. However, when they begin integrating, something shifts profoundly. The individual no longer lives only to endure the day.

Rather, they begin reconnecting with what matters, what nourishes, what inspires,

what heals, and what makes life emotionally worth inhabiting. This changes sleep deeply, for the nervous system no longer experiences life itself as constant depletion; and one of the most important truths about healing is this: rest is not merely recovery from work; rather, rest is reconnection with life.

This is why specific practices often profoundly affect sleep quality indirectly. These practices include gratitude, community, purpose, and service. These practices also include spirituality, creative expression, nature, mindfulness, and authentic relationships. They nourish the nervous system existentially, for the body softens when life begins feeling emotionally meaningful again.

At the SWEET Institute, we often encourage individuals to ask, “What kind of life would my nervous system no longer need to recover from constantly?” This question changes priorities, for sometimes healing sleep requires not only changing bedtime routines; rather, changing the way life itself is being lived. This does not mean abandoning responsibility. It means living with greater alignment, more intentionality, more humanity, more presence, more compassion, and more truth.

Throughout this book, we have explored how sleep emerges through the interaction of biology, attachment, trauma, emotion, conditioning, regulation, unconscious life, environment, and meaning across all four layers of transformation. The deeper realization becomes clear: Deep sleep is not merely physical unconsciousness. Deep sleep often reflects existential permission: the permission to stop striving temporarily; the permission to stop defending constantly; and the permission to stop surviving endlessly.

Deep sleep emerges when the nervous system finally believes, “Life is no longer only something to endure.” It emerges when the body begins trusting that it is allowed not only to survive life, but to fully live it.

The Exhaustion Spectrum

Burnout  Vitality

Selected Scientific References

- Frankl, V. E. (2006). *Man's search for meaning*. Beacon Press.
- Kabat-Zinn, J. (1990). *Full catastrophe living: Using the wisdom of your body and mind to face stress, pain, and illness*. Dell Publishing.
- Porges, S. W. (2011). *The polyvagal theory: Neurophysiological foundations of emotions, attachment, communication, and self-regulation*. W. W. Norton & Company.
- Siegel, D. J. (2012). *The developing mind: How relationships and the brain interact to shape who we are* (2nd ed.). Guilford Press.
- Steger, M. F. (2012). Making meaning in life. *Psychological Inquiry, 23*(4), 381–385. https://doi.org/10.1080/1047840X.2012.720832
- Van der Kolk, B. A. (2014). *The body keeps the score: Brain, mind, and body in the healing of trauma*. Viking.
- Walker, M. (2017). *Why we sleep: Unlocking the power of sleep and dreams*. Scribner.
- Yalom, I. D. (1980). *Existential psychotherapy*. Basic Books.

Chapter 24 — Deep Sleep: Integration, Freedom, and the Return to Self

At 6:14 a.m., Maya opened her eyes slowly. For the first time in years, she did not wake up already bracing for the day. Her body felt softer, her breathing felt deeper, and her mind felt quieter. Yet nothing in her life had become perfect. There were still responsibilities, still uncertainty, and still unresolved challenges. However, something fundamental had changed: Her nervous system no longer believed it had to remain at war with life.

At the SWEET Institute, we recognize that healing sleep is ultimately about far more than nighttime. Deep sleep reflects integration. Integration between body and mind, thought and emotion, past and present, self and others, behavior and meaning, awareness and unconscious life. Human beings suffer profoundly when these dimensions become fragmented.

In other words, the body says one thing, while the mind says another. The nervous system prepares for danger while conscious awareness insists, "Everything is fine." People continue functioning externally while internally exhausted. However, healing gradually reconnects what survival once forced apart. This is the essence of transformation.

At the biological domain of the SWEET Multi-Domain Model, healing sleep restores regulation across nearly every major physiological system, including immune functioning, emotional regulation, memory consolidation, and hormonal balance. It also restores metabolic restoration, cardiovascular recovery, attention, energy, and nervous system flexibility. The body begins recovering from years of chronic activation.

At the psychological domain, the individual slowly develops a different relationship with thought, emotion, and discomfort. Thoughts become less catastrophic; emotions become more tolerable; and stillness becomes less threatening. In other words, the nervous system becomes less reactive and more flexible at the relational domain, connection often deepens.

The individual becomes more emotionally present, less irritable, less defended, and less hypervigilant. Relationships soften because the nervous system no longer experiences constant threat. At the environmental domain, life itself becomes reorganized around rhythms that support regulation rather than chronic depletion.

Small, repeated choices create nervous system stability. They include sleep routines, boundaries, light exposure, and movement. They also include nutrition, technology use, restoration, and presence.

At the existential domain, perhaps the deepest transformation occurs: The individual begins reconnecting with self, with the deeper self that existed before endless adaptation, instead of the survival self, the performance self, the hypervigilant self, or the constantly proving self.

Research consistently demonstrates that long-term healing involves integration across biological, emotional, cognitive, relational, and existential dimensions simultaneously. Sustainable nervous system regulation emerges not through isolated interventions alone, but through repeated experiences of coherence, safety, meaning, flexibility, and connection. This is why healing sleep cannot be reduced to simple "tips." Human beings are layered.

At the conscious layer of transformation, individuals begin practicing new behaviors, including consistent routines, breath awareness, mindfulness, and emotional regulation.

These behaviors also include movement, boundaries, sleep hygiene, and compassionate self-care.

At the pre-conscious layer, deeper schemas gradually soften, "I am not safe." "I must always perform." "I cannot relax." "I am alone." "I must stay prepared." The nervous system slowly updates its emotional expectations.

At the unconscious layer, repressed emotional material gradually becomes integrated rather than endlessly defended against. Dreams become less terrifying; emotions become less overwhelming; and the body no longer has to carry so much unresolved burden silently.

At the existential layer, individuals begin reclaiming freedom, including freedom to rest, freedom to slow down, freedom to feel, freedom to exist without constant performance, and freedom to choose meaning intentionally. This is one reason deep sleep becomes symbolic. Deep sleep reflects trust; the nervous system trusts enough to let go; and for many individuals, this may be one of the deepest forms of healing imaginable, for chronic hypervigilance is exhausting, chronic striving is exhausting, chronic fear is exhausting; for the body was never designed to survive years of continuous activation without consequence.

At the SWEET Institute, we often emphasize that symptoms are not enemies. Symptoms are communication; insomnia communicates; exhaustion communicates; nightmares communicate; restlessness communicates; and hypervigilance communicates.

The body continuously attempts to protect the self. Healing begins the moment individuals stop attacking themselves for symptoms and begin listening compassionately to what the nervous system has been trying to communicate all along. This changes everything, for healing is no longer organized around self-war.

Healing becomes organized around relationship: relationship with the body, relationship with emotion, relationship with thought, and relationship with the unconscious. Healing also becomes organized around relationship with meaning, and relationship with self.

Throughout this book, we have explored circadian rhythm, sleep hygiene, environment, and technology. We have also explored dopamine, attachment, perfectionism, and trauma. Additional exploration has been around internal dialogue, core beliefs, breath awareness, and ritual, in addition to acceptance, dreams, repression, psychological safety, working through, and existential meaning.

However, underneath every chapter lives one central truth: The nervous system longs for safety, including emotional safety, relational safety, and existential safety. When the body gradually experiences enough safety, regulation emerges naturally, the mind quiets, the muscles soften, and the breathing slows. Further, the vigilance decreases, and the self-returns.

Nonetheless, this process is not linear. Some nights will still feel difficult, and some fears may still reappear, for healing unfolds in waves. However, the nervous system changes through repetition and every moment slowly reshapes the body's expectations about life itself. This includes a moment of awareness, compassion, regulation, and truth. This also includes a moment of connection, and integration.

At the SWEET Institute, we believe transformation occurs when individuals move through all four layers: conscious, pre-conscious, unconscious, and existential. This is integration; it is the return to wholeness; and perhaps that is the deepest truth about sleep: Deep sleep is not merely unconsciousness. It is what becomes possible when the body finally understands: We no longer have to survive every moment. We are allowed to rest. We are allowed to heal; and we are finally allowed to come home to ourselves.

The Existential Wheel

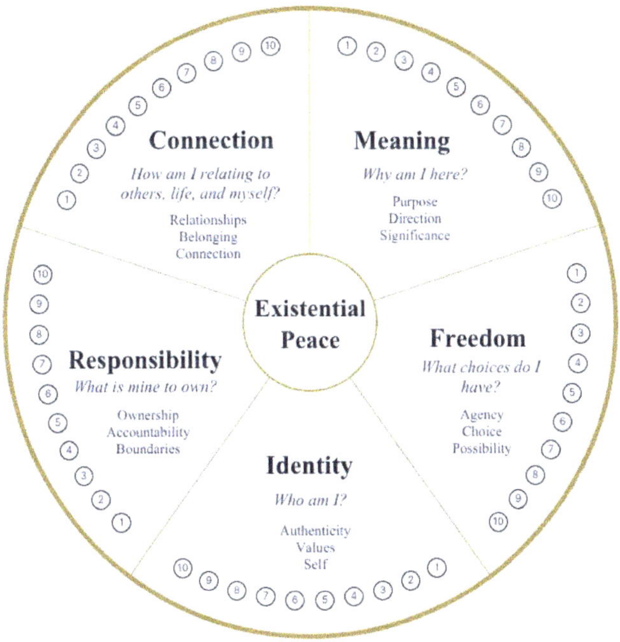

Each segment includes brief descriptors and a 1–10 self-rating scale to help identify which existential domain may be contributing most to exhaustion or sleep disruption.

Selected Scientific References

- Frankl, V. E. (2006). *Man's search for meaning*. Beacon Press.
- Hayes, S. C., Strosahl, K. D., & Wilson, K. G. (2016). *Acceptance and commitment therapy: The process and practice of mindful change* (2nd ed.). Guilford Press.
- Levine, P. A. (2010). *In an unspoken voice: How the body releases trauma and restores goodness*. North Atlantic Books.
- Perlis, M. L., Jungquist, C., Smith, M. T., & Posner, D. (2005). *Cognitive behavioral treatment of insomnia: A session-by-session guide*. Springer.
- Porges, S. W. (2011). *The polyvagal theory: Neurophysiological foundations of emotions, attachment, communication, and self-regulation*. W. W. Norton & Company.
- Siegel, D. J. (2012). *The developing mind: How relationships and the brain interact to shape who we are* (2nd ed.). Guilford Press.
- Van der Kolk, B. A. (2014). *The body keeps the score: Brain, mind, and body in the healing of trauma*. Viking.
- Walker, M. (2017). *Why we sleep: Unlocking the power of sleep and dreams*. Scribner.

Chapter 25 — The Deep Sleep Blueprint

At 9:58 p.m., Noah stood quietly in his kitchen holding a cup of tea. Months earlier, this hour would have looked very different: bright lights, phone in hand, television playing, and mind racing. It would have also looked like body tense, emotionally flooded, and trying desperately to "force" sleep later in the night. However, now something had shifted. The nervous system was finally learning another way to live.

At the SWEET Institute, we recognize that transformation becomes sustainable when insight turns into structure. People often understand what is hurting them. However, healing requires implementation, and this is why the Deep Sleep Blueprint exists.

It exists as a compassionate framework helping the nervous system relearn regulation, rhythm, flexibility, emotional safety, and restoration across all four layers of transformation. The blueprint is simple, but simple does not mean easy, for the nervous system changes through repeated experience, and what is repeated becomes strengthened.

At the biological domain of the SWEET Multi-Domain Model, the Deep Sleep Blueprint begins with rhythm, for the body thrives on consistency, and as such, wake time matters; morning light matters; movement matters; nutrition matters; hydration matters; and reducing overstimulation matters.

The body was designed around cycles: light and darkness; activation and restoration; and engagement and recovery. The first step of the Deep Sleep Blueprint is therefore: rebuild biological rhythm. This includes consistent wake times, morning sunlight exposure,

reduced evening stimulation, and regular movement. It also includes hydration, reduced late caffeine, moderate alcohol use, and creating environments supportive of nervous system regulation. The body slowly relearns predictability, and predictability creates safety.

At the conscious layer of transformation, behavioral awareness becomes essential. The individual begins asking, "What behaviors regulate my nervous system?" "What behaviors dysregulate it?" This is where the SWEET SDAF Framework becomes practical: Stabilize → Decide → Act → Feel.

Instead of impulsively reacting to discomfort, the individual pauses first, and makes use of breath awareness, grounding, movement, stillness, and compassion.

Then conscious choice becomes possible, and this changes nighttime profoundly, for the nervous system slowly becomes less reactive and more intentional.

At the psychological domain, the blueprint includes emotional awareness and cognitive flexibility. The individual begins recognizing catastrophic thinking, perfectionism, and hypervigilance. One also begins recognizing fear-based internal dialogue, and conditioned emotional patterns. Thoughts then stop being treated as absolute commands, and emotions stop being treated as emergencies. This creates psychological space, as the nervous system softens when internal threat signaling decreases.

At the pre-conscious layer, the Deep Sleep Blueprint includes identifying and gradually reshaping underlying schemas. Beliefs such as, "I must always stay alert." "I cannot relax." "I am only worthy when productive." "The world is unsafe." These beliefs profoundly affect physiology.

Healing therefore requires corrective emotional experiences, including safe relationships,

consistent routines, self-compassion, and boundary setting. These experiences also include rest without guilt, and learning that stillness can coexist with safety. The body updates its predictions gradually.

At the unconscious layer, the blueprint emphasizes emotional integration through dream reflection, free association, mindfulness, and journaling. It also emphasizes integration through therapy, body awareness, and emotional processing.

The goal is not endless analysis; rather, the goal is reducing the burden of unresolved emotional material continuously activating the nervous system beneath awareness. The unconscious mind no longer has to scream through symptoms when emotional experiences become integrated consciously.

At the existential layer, the Deep Sleep Blueprint becomes even deeper, for many individuals are not merely exhausted physically; rather, they are exhausted existentially. They are exhausted by disconnection, lack of meaning, constant performance, chronic urgency, or living lives misaligned with their deeper values.

The blueprint therefore includes purpose, connection, and presence. It includes play, contribution, creativity, and spirituality, in addition to gratitude, and meaningful relationships, for the nervous system regulates more deeply when life itself feels emotionally coherent.

This is the essence of the SWEET Body–Mind–Meaning Framework. The body needs regulation; the mind needs flexibility; meaning systems need alignment; and when these dimensions begin integrating, something profound occurs: The individual no longer approaches sleep as battle. Sleep then becomes relationship: relationship with the body, with emotion, and with self.

At the SWEET Institute, we often emphasize that sustainable transformation does not emerge through intensity alone; rather, it emerges through consistency, and small repeated actions matter more than occasional dramatic effort. Five minutes of breath awareness nightly; consistent wake times; and reduced nighttime stimulation. They also include gentler self-talk, morning sunlight, emotional honesty, and moments of stillness, in addition to repeated compassion.

The nervous system learns through accumulation, and this becomes especially important because healing is not linear. Some nights will still feel difficult. Stress will still exist. Old fears may still appear. However, now the individual responds differently, with awareness, with regulation, with flexibility, and with compassion; instead of panic, self-attack, or desperate control. In other words, the nervous system gradually becomes more resilient, and resilience changes sleep profoundly.

At the SWEET Institute, we believe transformation occurs through all four layers simultaneously: conscious, pre-conscious, unconscious, and existential. This is why true healing cannot be reduced to simple sleep hacks, for human beings are layered, and layered healing creates sustainable change.

The Deep Sleep Blueprint is therefore not simply a sleep plan; rather, it is a framework for rebuilding relationship with life itself. This includes a relationship where rest becomes allowed, stillness becomes survivable, emotion becomes tolerable, imperfection becomes human, and safety becomes increasingly internalized, for ultimately, deep sleep is not only about sleeping better; rather, deep sleep reflects something deeper: The nervous system no longer organizing around constant survival; and when that shift occurs, even gradually, the body begins remembering something it may not have experienced in years: Peace, and enough peace for the nervous system to finally release the day; enough peace for the mind to soften; enough peace for the body to trust the night again; enough peace to rest; and perhaps, enough peace to finally begin living fully awake.

THE DEEP SLEEP BLUEPRINT

A Practical Framework for Building Restorative Sleep

Deep Sleep

A body that feels safe enough to let go.

STEP 1

Regulate the Body

- Consistent wake time
- Morning sunlight
- Movement
- Reduce caffeine and alcohol
- Sleep-supportive environment

STEP 2

Calm the Mind

- Thought awareness
- Cognitive flexibility
- Reduce rumination
- Journaling
- Mindfulness

STEP 3

Heal Emotional Patterns

- Identify schemas
- Process unresolved emotions
- Understand attachment patterns
- Reduce emotional avoidance

STEP 4

Restore Safety

- Nervous system regulation
- Boundaries
- Relational safety
- Environmental safety

STEP 5

Reconnect with Meaning

- Purpose
- Values
- Joy
- Spirituality
- Authentic living

Selected Scientific References

- Frankl, V. E. (2006). *Man's search for meaning*. Beacon Press.
- Hayes, S. C., Strosahl, K. D., & Wilson, K. G. (2016). *Acceptance and commitment therapy: The process and practice of mindful change* (2nd ed.). Guilford Press.
- Kabat-Zinn, J. (1990). *Full catastrophe living: Using the wisdom of your body and mind to face stress, pain, and illness*. Dell Publishing.
- Perlis, M. L., Jungquist, C., Smith, M. T., & Posner, D. (2005). *Cognitive behavioral treatment of insomnia: A session-by-session guide*. Springer.
- Porges, S. W. (2011). *The polyvagal theory: Neurophysiological foundations of emotions, attachment, communication, and self-regulation*. W. W. Norton & Company.
- Siegel, D. J. (2012). *The developing mind: How relationships and the brain interact to shape who we are* (2nd ed.). Guilford Press.
- Van der Kolk, B. A. (2014). *The body keeps the score: Brain, mind, and body in the healing of trauma*. Viking.
- Walker, M. (2017). *Why we sleep: Unlocking the power of sleep and dreams*. Scribner.

Part VI – Integration and Transformation

Chapter 26 — The 30-Day Deep Sleep Transformation

At 10:07 p.m., Olivia sat quietly with her journal open beside her bed. Thirty days earlier, she felt hopeless. Her sleep was fragmented, her body was exhausted, her mind never stopped racing, and her nights felt like battles. Perhaps most painfully, she had started believing, "This is just who I am now."

However, over the past month, something subtle yet powerful had begun changing. Her nervous system was learning another way to exist.

At the SWEET Institute, we recognize that sustainable transformation does not emerge through dramatic intensity alone. Transformation emerges through repeated experience, and small shifts repeated consistently reshape physiology, emotional regulation, attention, identity, and nervous system expectation over time. This is why the near final section of Deep Sleep becomes deeply practical, for healing requires implementation, and the nervous system changes through lived experience.

Therefore, the 30-Day Deep Sleep Transformation is not a perfectionistic challenge. It is a compassionate re-training process helping the body relearn rhythm, regulation, safety,

flexibility, emotional integration, and restoration. The goal is not perfect sleep in thirty days; rather, the goal is building momentum toward nervous system healing.

At the biological domain of the SWEET Multi-Domain Model, the first phase of transformation focuses on restoring rhythm.

Days 1–7 emphasize:

- consistent wake times,
- morning sunlight exposure,
- hydration,
- gentle movement,
- reducing evening stimulation,

- and beginning environmental regulation.

The purpose is not immediate perfection; rather, the purpose is helping the nervous system re-establish predictability, for the body learns through repetition.

During this phase, individuals are encouraged to observe without judgment. They are encouraged to observe without judgment, energy patterns, caffeine intake, screen use, nighttime activation, emotional triggers, and sleep rhythms, for awareness itself becomes transformative.

At the conscious layer of transformation, Days 8–14 focus on behavioral regulation and nervous system calming.

This phase includes:

- creating bedtime rituals,
- reducing late-night stimulation,
- practicing breath awareness,
- limiting doom scrolling,
- decreasing self-attack,
- and introducing intentional pauses throughout the day.

The individual begins practicing the SWEET SDAF Framework:

Stabilize → Decide → Act → Feel.

This interrupts automatic coping patterns, and the nervous system slowly becomes less reactive and more intentional.

At the psychological domain, Days 15–21 focus on internal dialogue and emotional awareness.

This phase invites reflection around:

- perfectionism,
- catastrophic thinking,
- fear of rest,
- hyper-responsibility,
- attachment patterns,
- and emotional avoidance.

Journaling becomes important here.

Questions include:

- "What does my nervous system fear at night?"
- "What internal dialogue keeps me activated?"
- "What emotions appear when I slow down?"
- "What am I continuously trying to outrun?"

This phase often becomes emotional for many individuals because stillness begins exposing deeper layers previously hidden beneath stimulation and survival routines.

At the pre-conscious layer, Days 22–26 focus on identifying deeper schemas and conditioned emotional beliefs.

Individuals begin exploring questions such as:

- "What did I learn about safety growing up?"
- "What did I learn about rest?"
- "What did I learn about vulnerability?"
- "What did I learn about worth and productivity?"
- "What does my body still expect from life?"

The nervous system often carries beliefs long after conscious awareness evolves; and healing requires helping the body experience corrective emotional reality repeatedly.

This includes:

- rest without guilt,
- slowing without catastrophe,
- emotional honesty,
- safe connection,
- and compassionate flexibility.

At the unconscious layer, Days 27–29 invite deeper reflection around dreams, emotional patterns, symbolic themes, recurring fears, and unresolved emotional experiences.

This phase includes:

- dream journaling,
- free association,
- mindfulness,
- body awareness,
- and emotional curiosity.

The goal is not obsessive analysis. The goal is relationship with the unconscious rather than chronic avoidance of it. Many individuals discover that insomnia itself carried emotional meaning all along. The nervous system was not broken; rather, it was communicating.

Finally, at the existential layer, Day 30 becomes integration.

The individual reflects not only on sleep, but on life itself.

Questions include:

- "What kind of life supports nervous system peace?"
- "What relationships nourish regulation?"
- "What environments dysregulate me?"
- "What values matter most?"
- "What does my body need more of?"
- "What does my soul need more of?"

Because ultimately, healing sleep is not merely about nighttime. It is about how life itself is being lived.

At the SWEET Institute, we often emphasize that nervous systems regulate most deeply when body, mind, and meaning begin aligning again.

This is the essence of the SWEET Body–Mind–Meaning Framework. The body needs rhythm. The mind needs flexibility. Meaning systems need coherence. And when these dimensions begin reconnecting, the nervous system gradually stops organizing around chronic survival.

One of the most important truths about transformation is this: Progress is often quieter than people expect. Healing may initially appear as slightly softer mornings, slightly calmer evenings, and less catastrophic thinking. It may also initially appear as more awareness, gentler self-talk, more emotional honesty, or brief moments of stillness becoming tolerable.

These moments matter enormously, for as we've emphasized countless times, the nervous system changes through accumulation.

At the SWEET Institute, we encourage individuals not to measure healing only by whether sleep was "perfect." Rather, we encourage them to ask, "Am I becoming more regulated?" "Am I becoming more compassionate with myself?" "Am I becoming less reactive?" "Am I becoming more connected to life?"

These shifts often precede deeper sleep itself, and over time, the body begins responding differently. The muscles soften more easily. The mind quiets more quickly, and fear decreases. The nervous system releases vigilance more consistently, and the body relearns restoration. This process is deeply human and profoundly possible.

Throughout Deep Sleep, we have explored the four layers of transformation:

- conscious,
- pre-conscious,
- unconscious,
- and existential.

We have explored biology, psychology, attachment, trauma, meaning, dreams, regulation, ritual, emotional conditioning, perfectionism, and nervous system healing.

Now, perhaps the deepest truth remains: The body has always been trying to heal. Symptoms were communication. Exhaustion was communication. Insomnia was communication. The nervous system was never trying to punish the individua; rather, it was trying to survive; and healing begins the moment survival no longer becomes the only mode of existence available.

Deep sleep emerges gradually when the body finally experiences enough safety to release chronic preparation; and perhaps this is the greatest transformation of all: it is not merely sleeping more deeply, but living more deeply, feeling more deeply, connecting more deeply, existing more honestly, and finally returning, not to perfection, but to wholeness.

Purpose and Restoration

Body–Mind–Meaning Framework

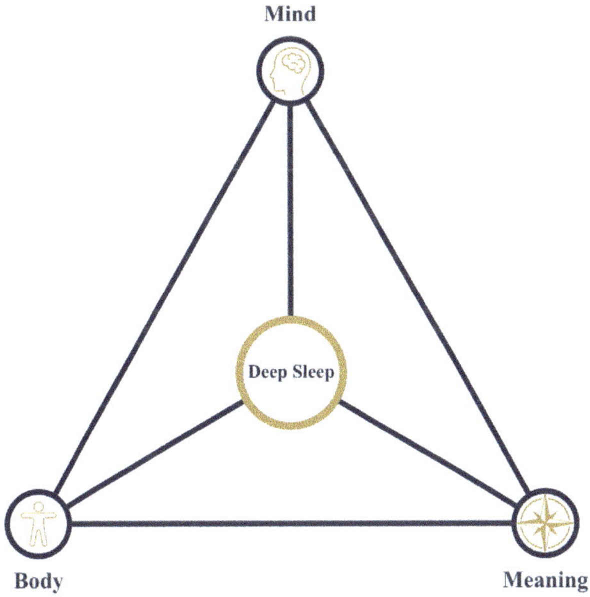

Selected Scientific References

- Frankl, V. E. (2006). *Man's search for meaning*. Beacon Press.
- Hayes, S. C., Strosahl, K. D., & Wilson, K. G. (2016). *Acceptance and commitment therapy: The process and practice of mindful change* (2nd ed.). Guilford Press.
- Kabat-Zinn, J. (1990). *Full catastrophe living: Using the wisdom of your body and mind to face stress, pain, and illness*. Dell Publishing.
- Perlis, M. L., Jungquist, C., Smith, M. T., & Posner, D. (2005). *Cognitive behavioral treatment of insomnia: A session-by-session guide*. Springer.
- Porges, S. W. (2011). *The polyvagal theory: Neurophysiological foundations of emotions, attachment, communication, and self-regulation*. W. W. Norton & Company.
- Siegel, D. J. (2012). *The developing mind: How relationships and the brain interact to shape who we are* (2nd ed.). Guilford Press.
- Van der Kolk, B. A. (2014). *The body keeps the score: Brain, mind, and body in the healing of trauma*. Viking.
- Walker, M. (2017). *Why we sleep: Unlocking the power of sleep and dreams*. Scribner.

Chapter 27 — The Future of Sleep, Healing, and Human Consciousness

At 11:11 p.m., Jordan looked around the city from his apartment window. Lights everywhere; phones glowing; and notifications vibrating.

People were awake, working, scrolling, consuming, and performing. The world no longer slept the way it once did; and perhaps, he thought quietly, humanity itself had become exhausted in ways deeper than anyone fully understood.

At the SWEET Institute, we recognize that sleep is not merely an individual issue. Sleep has become a cultural issue, a relational issue, a technological issue, ad an existential issue.

Modern society continuously rewards overstimulation while simultaneously punishing restoration. People are praised for working constantly, answering immediately,

remaining available endlessly, producing continuously, and overriding biological limitation.

Rest increasingly becomes associated with laziness. Stillness becomes associated with weakness. Silence becomes intolerable, and the nervous system pays the price.

At the biological domain of the SWEET Multi-Domain Model, humanity now faces unprecedented levels of circadian disruption, technological overstimulation, chronic stress activation, social fragmentation, sleep deprivation, emotional overload, and nervous system dysregulation. Artificial light extends daytime indefinitely. Technology competes aggressively for attention. Stress follows people home continuously; and the nervous system rarely experiences true psychological endings.

Research increasingly demonstrates that chronic sleep deprivation is associated not only with anxiety and depression, but also with cardiovascular disease, metabolic dysfunction, impaired immunity, cognitive decline, emotional dysregulation, burnout, reduced empathy, impaired decision-making, and decreased overall well-being. The consequences extend far beyond fatigue, for sleep deprivation changes how human beings think, feel, relate, and exist.

At the psychological domain, many individuals no longer know how to slow down without feeling emotionally uncomfortable. Stillness exposes emotional overload previously hidden beneath stimulation. The mind remains conditioned toward constant distraction, and the nervous system becomes addicted to activation.

This creates a profound paradox: People desperately long for peace. Yet many simultaneously fear the silence where peace begins.

At the conscious layer, behavior is visible, and individuals can observe habits, thoughts, emotions, and routines. They may also recognize that late-night scrolling, inconsistent schedules, chronic work demands, or emotional stress are affecting their sleep.

However, awareness alone, his rarely sufficient.

Most people know quality sleep is essential, and they understand the importance of sleep hygiene. Yet knowledge without deeper transformation often produces frustration rather than lasting change.

Within the SWEET Model, the conscious layer is where insight begins. However, sustainable healing requires moving beneath awareness into the pre-conscious beliefs, unconscious protective adaptations, and existential meanings that continue shaping behavior.

At the pre-conscious layer, modern culture reinforces schemas organized around:

productivity, urgency, performance, optimization, comparison, and endless achievement.

Individuals internalize beliefs such as, "My worth depends on output." "If I stop, I fall behind." "Rest must be earned." "I must always remain available." These beliefs become nervous system realities, and the body eventually collapses under chronic pressure.

At the unconscious layer, many modern coping systems function defensively. Technology distracts from emotional pain. Endless stimulation prevents emotional contact; and busyness protects against vulnerability. Performance protects against shame; consumption protects against emptiness; and the unconscious mind continuously searches for ways to avoid emotional overwhelm. However, avoidance itself often deepens exhaustion, the nervous system remains disconnected from genuine restoration.

At the existential layer, humanity increasingly confronts a profound question: What kind of life are modern nervous systems trying to survive? This question may become one of the defining psychological questions of the future, for human beings cannot endlessly override biology without consequence. The body eventually communicates through burnout, insomnia, anxiety, and depression. The body also communicates through hypervigilance, exhaustion, numbness, disconnection, or emotional collapse. In other words, symptoms become messages.

At the SWEET Institute, we believe the future of healing will increasingly require integration rather than fragmentation. The future cannot rely only on symptom suppression, for human beings are layered, Biological, Psychological, Relational, Environmental, and Existential; and sustainable healing must address all domains simultaneously.

This is why the future of sleep medicine itself may need expansion, beyond medication alone, beyond sleep hygiene alone, and toward integrated nervous system healing, toward trauma-informed care, and toward attachment-informed models. The future of sleep medicine itself may need expansion toward mindfulness and regulation, toward emotional integration, toward meaning, toward relational safety, and toward helping individuals reconnect with the body itself.

In fact, the future of neuroscience increasingly points toward integration: neuroplasticity,

polyvagal theory, mindfulness research, and attachment science. It also increasingly points toward trauma research, behavioral sleep medicine, emotion regulation, and the embodied nature of psychological experience. The body and mind are not separate, and sleep reflects this truth profoundly.

At the SWEET Institute, we believe the future of healing will increasingly involve helping people move through all four layers of transformation: conscious, pre-conscious, unconscious, and existential; for symptoms often persist when deeper layers remain unaddressed. Behavior matters, and meaning matters too. Thoughts matter, and relationships matter too. Biology matters, and emotional history matters too.

Perhaps one of the most revolutionary truths of all is this: Human beings do not heal through information alone. They heal through experience. They heal through repeated experiences of safety, connection, presence, and regulation. They also heal through repeated experiences of compassion, truth, flexibility, and meaning. The nervous system changes through lived reality.

This is why the future of healing may depend less on teaching people how to "perform wellness" and more on helping them create lives their nervous systems no longer need to recover from constantly. In this vein, sleep is no longer viewed merely as a productivity tool, a recovery mechanism, or a biological necessity.

Sleep also becomes sacred, a return, and a recalibration. It becomes a restoration of relationship between body, mind, and meaning.

At the SWEET Institute, we often say: The body whispers before it screams. Sleep disturbance is often one of the first whispers. The nervous system is communicating that something is overloaded, something is unresolved, something is disconnected, and something is unsustainable.

Perhaps the future of healing begins the moment humanity finally starts listening to the body, emotion, relationship, silence, meaning, and the wisdom hidden beneath chronic overstimulation, for deep sleep is not merely about unconsciousness; rather, it may ultimately become one of the clearest reflections of whether human beings are living in alignment with their biology, psychology, relationships, environments, and deeper humanity. The greatest transformation of all may not simply be helping people sleep better; rather, it may be helping humanity remember how to live differently; slower, softer, more connected, more aware, more present, more human, and maybe, finally, more awake.

Return to Self

The Healing Journey

Selected Scientific References

- Cacioppo, J. T., & Patrick, W. (2008). *Loneliness: Human nature and the need for social connection*. W. W. Norton & Company.
- Frankl, V. E. (2006). *Man's search for meaning*. Beacon Press.
- Kabat-Zinn, J. (1990). *Full catastrophe living: Using the wisdom of your body and mind to face stress, pain, and illness*. Dell Publishing.
- Porges, S. W. (2011). *The polyvagal theory: Neurophysiological foundations of emotions, attachment, communication, and self-regulation*. W. W. Norton & Company.
- Siegel, D. J. (2012). *The developing mind: How relationships and the brain interact to shape who we are* (2nd ed.). Guilford Press.
- Twenge, J. M. (2017). *iGen: Why today's super-connected kids are growing up less rebellious, more tolerant, less happy—and completely unprepared for adulthood*. Atria Books.
- Van der Kolk, B. A. (2014). *The body keeps the score: Brain, mind, and body in the healing of trauma*. Viking.
- Walker, M. (2017). *Why we sleep: Unlocking the power of sleep and dreams*. Scribner.

Chapter 28 — Awakening: Living Beyond Survival

At 6:42 a.m., Sofia stepped outside before the city fully awakened. The air felt cool, the sky slowly brightened, and for the first time in years, she noticed something she had almost forgotten: Silence did not feel dangerous anymore. There was no urgent need to check her phone, no immediate rush to escape herself, and no panic rising in her chest.

There was just breath, just presence, and just the quiet realization that healing had changed more than her sleep, for healing had changed her relationship with life itself.

At the SWEET Institute, we recognize that true transformation eventually moves beyond symptom reduction. People often begin healing because they want relief: better sleep, less anxiety, less exhaustion, or less suffering.

However, as the nervous system gradually regulates, something deeper often emerges. Awareness. The individual begins realizing how long survival mode shaped nearly every part of life. The individual begins realizing how long fear organized decisions, how long hypervigilance shaped relationships, how long perfectionism drove behavior, and how long exhaustion disconnected them from joy, stillness, intimacy, creativity, meaning, and self. Perhaps most importantly, the individual begins realizing how much of life had been lived bracing rather than fully living.

At the existential domain of the SWEET Multi-Domain Model, healing ultimately becomes an awakening process, and not awakening in a mystical sense, but awakening into greater contact with reality. It is a greater contact with the body, emotion, and relationship. It is a greater contact with meaning, choice, freedom, and presence. The nervous system slowly stops organizing around chronic defense; and this changes consciousness itself.

Research increasingly demonstrates that chronic stress, sleep deprivation, trauma, hypervigilance, and emotional overload narrow attention, reduce psychological flexibility, impair emotional regulation, and alter perception itself. Exhausted nervous systems experience the world differently; healing changes perception, and this is profoundly important.

At the biological domain, the body begins recovering from years of activation. Inflammation decreases, restoration improves, and emotional flexibility increases.

Attention also stabilizes, and energy deepens. In other words, the nervous system becomes more resilient and less reactive.

At the psychological domain, the mind gradually softens. Catastrophic thinking decreases, emotional tolerance increases, and thoughts become less fused with identity. The individual no longer experiences every uncertainty as immediate danger.

At the relational domain, connection deepens. People become more emotionally available, more compassionate, more authentic, and more capable of intimacy without constant self-protection. In other words, relationships begin feeling less like survival and more like genuine connection.

At the environmental domain, the individual begins intentionally creating a life supportive of regulation rather than chronic depletion. Boundaries become clearer, technology becomes more intentional, rest becomes valued, and rhythm returns.

At the existential domain, perhaps the deepest shift occurs: The individual stops living only reactively, life becomes more conscious, more chosen, and more aligned. This is why healing sleep often becomes symbolic of something larger.

Deep sleep reflects trust: trust in the body, trust in the nervous system, and trust that one no longer has to remain endlessly prepared for catastrophe. For many individuals, this trust may feel revolutionary, for survival mode often becomes identity.

People become accustomed to overthinking, overworking, overpreparing, overperforming, and overriding the body continuously. Hypervigilance begins feeling normal, exhaustion begins feeling normal, and disconnection begins feeling normal.

One day, then, regulation returns just enough for the individual to realize, "This was never truly living."

At the SWEET Institute, we often emphasize that awakening begins when individuals stop organizing life entirely around fear, for fear no longer controls every decision, and the nervous system becomes flexible enough to remain open even in the presence of uncertainty.

This changes life profoundly because now the individual can begin choosing presence over urgency, connection over performance, and restoration over endless stimulation. The individual can also begin choosing truth over avoidance, and meaning over survival alone. Healing therefore becomes not only symptom reduction. Healing becomes liberation. Liberation from automatic patterns, chronic self-attack, endless emotional avoidance, and the belief that worth must always be earned through exhaustion.

This is why deep sleep ultimately reflects freedom. The body no longer needs to stay prepared every moment. The nervous system releases chronic defense; and the individual begins returning to something deeply human: aliveness, which, in turn, is the ability to feel deeply, rest deeply, and love deeply, Aliveness is also the ability to grieve honestly, exist authentically, and remain present without constantly escaping the moment.

This is what many exhausted people are truly longing for. They are not longing simply for more sleep; rather, they are longing for reconnection with themselves.

At the SWEET Institute, we believe transformation occurs through all four layers simultaneously: conscious, pre-conscious, unconscious, and existential.

Behavior changes matter; schema work matters; emotional integration matters; and meaning matters, for human beings are layered, and sustainable healing must honor the whole person.

Throughout Deep Sleep, we have explored biology, circadian rhythm, nervous system, and regulation. We have also explored trauma, attachment, dreams, and repression, in addition to internal dialogue, technology, ritual, and breath awareness. Psychological safety, acceptance, purpose, and existential meaning have also been explored. However, underneath every chapter lives one essential truth: The body has always been trying to guide the individual back toward wholeness.

Symptoms were communication; exhaustion was communication; insomnia was communication; and the nervous system was never broken; rather, it was adapting, and now, through awareness, compassion, regulation, truth, and integration, another possibility emerges: The individual no longer has to spend life merely surviving.

They can begin living awake. They can begin awake to their body, their relationships, their patterns, and their meaning. They can also begin awake to their choices, their humanity, and their deeper self; and perhaps this is the final paradox of Deep Sleep: When people finally learn how to rest deeply, they often begin living more fully awake than ever before, for deep sleep is not the opposite of awakening.

Deep sleep may actually become one of the pathways leading toward it, and maybe that is what healing was always about, and finally becoming safe enough to return to who we were beneath the fear all along.

The Four Layers Working Together

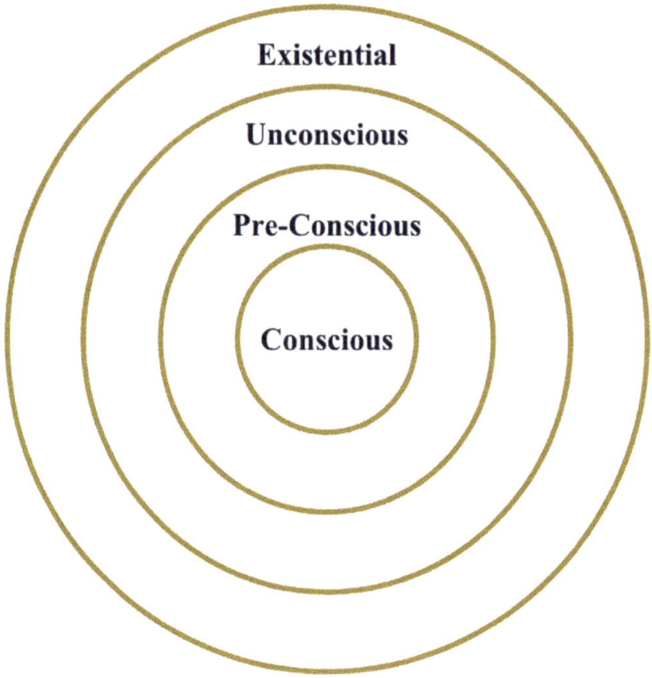

Selected Scientific References

- Frankl, V. E. (2006). *Man's search for meaning*. Beacon Press.
- Hayes, S. C., Strosahl, K. D., & Wilson, K. G. (2016). *Acceptance and commitment therapy: The process and practice of mindful change* (2nd ed.). Guilford Press.
- Kabat-Zinn, J. (1990). *Full catastrophe living: Using the wisdom of your body and mind to face stress, pain, and illness*. Dell Publishing.
- Porges, S. W. (2011). *The polyvagal theory: Neurophysiological foundations of emotions, attachment, communication, and self-regulation*. W. W. Norton & Company.
- Siegel, D. J. (2012). *The developing mind: How relationships and the brain interact to shape who we are* (2nd ed.). Guilford Press.
- Van der Kolk, B. A. (2014). *The body keeps the score: Brain, mind, and body in the healing of trauma*. Viking.
- Walker, M. (2017). *Why we sleep: Unlocking the power of sleep and dreams*. Scribner.
- Yalom, I. D. (1980). *Existential psychotherapy*. Basic Books.

Chapter 29 — The Nightly Return: A Guided Practice for Deep Sleep

At 10:46 p.m., Ava turned off the final light in her apartment. For years, nighttime had filled her with dread, and the moment the world became quiet, her mind became loud. Thoughts raced, emotions surfaced, her body tightened, and sleep felt impossibly far away. However, tonight was different. Life had not become perfect, but she had stopped fighting herself.

At the SWEET Institute, we recognize that healing often requires ritual. The nervous system responds deeply to repeated emotional experiences. Ritual creates rhythm, rhythm creates predictability, predictability creates safety, and safety allows the nervous system to release vigilance.

This is why this chapter of Deep Sleep becomes a guided nightly return, a return to the body, a return to awareness, and a return to regulation. It is also a return to presence, and a return to self.

At the biological domain of the SWEET Multi-Domain Model, the nervous system transitions more effectively into sleep when stimulation decreases gradually rather than abruptly. The body was not designed to move directly from high activation into deep restoration instantly. Transition matters.

This is why the first phase of the nightly return begins one hour before intended sleep. Lights soften, stimulation decreases, technology becomes limited, and the nervous system begins receiving the message, "The day is ending." This simple transition profoundly affects physiology.

At the conscious layer of transformation, individuals are encouraged to pause intentionally before bed and ask, "What state is my nervous system currently in?" Am I activated? I am emotionally flooded? Restless? Numb? Disconnected? They are also encouraged to pause and ask: Am I overstimulated? Lonely? Fearful? Exhausted? For awareness interrupts automaticity, and the individual stops unconsciously carrying the day directly into the night.

At the SWEET Institute, we often encourage beginning with breath awareness, simply noticing it, noticing the inhale, the exhale, the body softening slowly, with a simple reminder, "I am here." The nervous system begins orienting toward the present moment instead of remaining trapped in anticipatory fear.

At the psychological domain, the nightly return includes emotional honesty. Many individuals attempt to suppress emotional reality all day long, but suppression increases activation. Instead, individuals are encouraged to ask gently, "What emotions am I carrying tonight?" Fear? Sadness? Pressure? Or Loneliness? They are encouraged to ask gently: Anger? Overwhelm? Grief? Uncertainty? The goal is not emotional flooding; rather, the goal is emotional acknowledgment, for the nervous system softens when emotions no longer need to fight for recognition.

At the pre-conscious layer, the nightly return includes observing internal dialogue compassionately. What is the mind communicating? "Tomorrow will be terrible." "You are failing." "You are unsafe." "You cannot relax." Rather than automatically believing these thoughts, the individual practices cognitive flexibility. "I notice this fear." "I notice this pressure." "I notice this activation." Awareness creates space, and the nervous system experiences less threat when thoughts are observed rather than fused with completely.

At the unconscious layer, the nightly return invites gentle openness rather than emotional avoidance. Dreams may come; feelings may surface; and memories may arise. The individual no longer treats internal experience as enemy. Instead, the body slowly learns:

"We can remain present safely." This becomes deeply regulating.

At the existential layer, the nightly return becomes more than preparation for sleep. It becomes reconnection with humanity itself. Yet the modern world rarely encourages stillness. People move constantly; consume constantly; and react constantly. However, nighttime offers another possibility: silence, reflection, presence, and meaning.

The individual begins remembering, "I do not exist only to produce." "I do not need to earn rest." "I am allowed to soften;" and this realization changes the nervous system profoundly.

At the SWEET Institute, we often encourage a simple closing reflection each night, "What does my body need from me right now?" Sometimes the answer is: stillness, compassion, slowing down, or grief. Other times the answer is: boundaries, forgiveness, connection, or simply permission to stop carrying everything for one night.

The nervous system regulates through listening, and this is why self-compassion becomes biologically important. Shame activates the nervous system; compassion regulates it; and one of the most powerful practices in the nightly return is therefore gentle self-talk.

Instead of, "I must sleep immediately." The individual practices, "My nervous system is learning safety." Instead of, "What is wrong with me?" The individual practices, "My body has been trying to protect me." Instead of, "I am failing." The individual practices: "Healing takes repetition." The nervous system listens continuously to emotional tone.

At the biological domain, additional practices may include cooling the room, soft lighting, gentle stretching, and warm showers. They may also include consistent sleep times, reduced late eating, and calming sensory experiences. These practices support regulation physically.

At the relational domain, safe connection also matters profoundly: a calm conversation, a hug, a sense of emotional safety, and shared presence. Human nervous systems regulate relationally, and the body softens when connection feels safe.

At the environmental domain, individuals are encouraged to create physical spaces supportive of restoration rather than stimulation. The bedroom becomes associated not with performance, panic, or endless scrolling, but with safety and restoration.

And at the existential domain, the nightly return ultimately becomes an act of trust. Trust that the body can release. Trust that life can pause temporarily. Trust that uncertainty can exist without immediate catastrophe. This trust develops slowly, but repetition matters.

At the SWEET Institute, we often emphasize that healing is not one dramatic moment. Healing is accumulated experience, one regulated evening at a time, one compassionate pause at a time, ne softened breath at a time, and one honest moment at a time.

Gradually, the nervous system begins believing something it may not have believed for years, "We are finally safe enough to rest." Perhaps this is the deepest purpose of the nightly return: not simply to fall asleep, but to help the individual stop abandoning themselves long enough to finally come home internally.

Deep sleep is not merely physical unconsciousness. It is what emerges when the body, mind, and meaning no longer remain fragmented from one another. It is the nervous system remembering how to trust the night again. Perhaps, in learning how to trust the night, human beings slowly begin learning how to trust life itself.

Return to Rest

The Deep Sleep Formula

Selected Scientific References

- Hayes, S. C., Strosahl, K. D., & Wilson, K. G. (2016). *Acceptance and commitment therapy: The process and practice of mindful change* (2nd ed.). Guilford Press.
- Kabat-Zinn, J. (1990). *Full catastrophe living: Using the wisdom of your body and mind to face stress, pain, and illness*. Dell Publishing.
- Levine, P. A. (2010). *In an unspoken voice: How the body releases trauma and restores goodness*. North Atlantic Books.
- Perlis, M. L., Jungquist, C., Smith, M. T., & Posner, D. (2005). *Cognitive behavioral treatment of insomnia: A session-by-session guide*. Springer.
- Porges, S. W. (2011). *The polyvagal theory: Neurophysiological foundations of emotions, attachment, communication, and self-regulation*. W. W. Norton & Company.
- Siegel, D. J. (2012). *The developing mind: How relationships and the brain interact to shape who we are* (2nd ed.). Guilford Press.
- Van der Kolk, B. A. (2014). *The body keeps the score: Brain, mind, and body in the healing of trauma*. Viking.
- Walker, M. (2017). *Why we sleep: Unlocking the power of sleep and dreams*. Scribner.

Conclusion

Deep Sleep Is Not About Sleep

If you remember only one thing from this book, let it be this: Deep sleep is not about sleep. At least not only about sleep for sleep is the symptom, the messenger, the mirror, and often the place where the body tells the truth.

Throughout these pages, we have explored circadian rhythms, sleep hygiene, light exposure, technology, nutrition, caffeine, and alcohol. We have explored movement, nervous system regulation, attachment, trauma, and internal dialogue in core beliefs. Lastly, we have explored dreams, emotional suppression, psychological safety, meaning, purpose, and human consciousness.

At first glance, these topics may seem unrelated. However, they are all connected by one central reality: The human nervous system is always asking the same question. Am I safe enough to let go?

That question sits beneath sleep, beneath anxiety, beneath hypervigilance, and beneath perfectionism. That question sits beneath overthinking, beneath burnout, beneath emotional exhaustion, and beneath so much of human suffering.

For years, many people approach sleep as a battle. They fight their thoughts, their emotions, their bodies and their past. They also fight the night and themselves. Yet healing rarely occurs through fighting; rather, it occurs through understanding. In other words, the body does not need more war. It needs more safety, more regulation, more compassion, and more integration.

This is why the Four Layers of Transformation matter so deeply.

At the conscious layer, we change behaviors. At the pre-conscious layer, we change patterns. At the unconscious layer, we integrate what has been hidden; and at the existential layer, we reclaim meaning.

When these layers work together, transformation becomes sustainable, for while life does not become perfect, the individual becomes more integrated, more whole, more aligned and freer.

Throughout this book, we have also explored the SWEET Multi-Domain Model. Every human experience occurs simultaneously across the Biological, Psychological, Relational, Environmental, and Existential domains. Sleep is no exception. A sleeping pill may help biology, but if relationships remain unsafe, the nervous system may stay activated.

A perfect bedtime routine may help behavior, but if unresolved grief remains untouched, the body may still struggle to rest. An optimized bedroom may support restoration, but if life itself has become disconnected from meaning, exhaustion may persist. True healing requires us to see the whole person, and not just the symptom, or the diagnosis, or just the sleep problem, rather, the whole person.

This is also why the SWEET Body–Mind–Meaning Framework is so important. The body needs regulation. The mind needs flexibility; and meaning needs coherence. When one is neglected, suffering increases. When all three begin working together, restoration becomes possible.

People believe they need more productivity, more optimization, or more efficiency. They also believe that they need more performance. Yet this is the greatest misunderstanding in modern culture for often what they really need is permission, permission to rest, to slow down, and to feel. They also need permission to grieve, to heal, and to be human.

As such, before you close this book, we invite you to consider a few final questions. What has your body been trying to tell you? What has your exhaustion been trying to teach you? What part of your life needs more attention? What part of your nervous system needs more compassion? What are you carrying that no longer belongs to you? What would change if you stopped treating yourself like a problem to be solved and started treating yourself like a human being worthy of care?

These questions matter because sleep is not simply something that happens at night. Rather, it is influenced by how we live during the day, including how we think, how we love and how we work. It is also influenced by how we cope, how we heal, and how we relate to ourselves.

Furthermore, perhaps the deepest truth of all is this: The body has never stopped moving toward healing. The nervous system has never stopped trying to protect you; and even your symptoms have been attempts at adaptation. In other words, the problem is not that your nervous system learned survival. The problem is that many of us never learned how to move beyond it.

That is the invitation of this book: to move beyond survival, to move toward regulation, and to move toward integration. It is the invitation to move toward meaning, toward wholeness and toward peace.

Human life will always contain uncertainty. There will always be challenges, losses, transitions, heartbreaks, or unexpected turns. However, there is a profound difference between experiencing life from a regulated nervous system and experiencing life from a chronically activated one.

A regulated nervous system does not eliminate suffering. It transforms our relationship with suffering, and that changes everything.

As you leave these pages, our hope is not simply that you sleep better. Our hope is that you live differently. Our hope is that you listen more carefully to your body, more compassionate toward yourself, and that you slow down enough to hear what your nervous system has been saying all along.

Our hope is also that you learn to create a life that supports restoration rather than constantly demanding recovery; and that, little by little, night after night, breath after breath, choice after choice, you rediscover something that exhaustion may have convinced you was lost: your capacity for peace, for deep sleep is not merely the absence of wakefulness. Deep sleep is what becomes possible when the body, mind, and meaning of a life begin working together again.

Deep sleep is the nervous system remembering safety, the mind releasing struggle, the body trusting the night, and the return of rest.

Ultimately, perhaps, deep sleep is the return of you.

Sleep well. Live deeply. And remember, healing is possible.

Mardoche Sidor, MD
Karen Dubin, Ph.D., LCSW
The SWEET Institute

An Invitation to the Reader

If you have reached this page, we would first like to thank you. Thank you for investing your time, attention, energy, and trust in this journey. Of all the books you could have chosen, of all the demands competing for your attention, you chose to spend some of your precious time with these pages. We do not take that lightly.

Whether you came to this book because you struggle with sleep, care for someone who does, work in the helping professions, or simply wish to understand yourself more deeply, we hope this journey has been meaningful. More importantly, we hope it has reminded you of something essential: you are not broken. You are not failing. You are not weak because you struggle. You are human. And being human means carrying burdens, adapting to challenges, learning from experience, healing from wounds, and continuously becoming.

Our hope is that this book has done more than help you sleep. We hope it has helped you listen more carefully to your body, understand your nervous system more compassionately, and reconnect with parts of yourself that may have been neglected, ignored, or forgotten. We hope it has helped you see that many of the symptoms you have struggled against were not signs of weakness, but signs of a nervous system doing its very best to protect you.

At the SWEET Institute, we believe that transformation occurs when knowledge becomes experience and experience becomes action. Reading a book can open a door, but walking through that door requires practice. For that reason, we invite you not to leave these ideas on the page. Choose one insight that resonated with you. Choose one practice that felt meaningful. Choose one habit that you are willing to strengthen. Then begin there.

You do not need to transform your entire life overnight. In fact, lasting transformation rarely occurs that way. Sustainable change is usually the result of small actions repeated consistently over time: one breath, one decision, one evening, one act of self-compassion, and one moment of awareness. These small moments accumulate: they shape habits, habits shape identity, and identity shapes destiny.

As you move forward, we encourage you to remain curious. Continue noticing what helps your nervous system feel safe. Continue paying attention to the relationship between your body, your thoughts, your emotions, your relationships, your environment, and your sense of meaning. Continue asking what your body might be trying to communicate rather than assuming it is working against you.

You may find that the greatest gift of this journey is not simply better sleep. You may discover greater patience, deeper self-awareness, stronger relationships, increased emotional flexibility, and a more compassionate relationship with yourself. You may discover that sleep was never the destination, rather, it was the doorway.

Before you close this book, we invite you to pause for a moment and reflect. What is the most important insight you are taking with you? What is one change you are ready to make? What would become possible if your nervous system felt safer, calmer, and more regulated six months from now? Allow yourself to sit with these questions. Sometimes the answers that change our lives emerge not from rushing forward, but from slowing down long enough to listen.

Finally, we would like to ask a small favor. If this book has been meaningful to you, we would be deeply grateful if you would consider leaving a review. Reviews help other readers discover resources that may support their own healing journeys. Even a few sentences sharing your experience can make an enormous difference.

On behalf of all of us at the SWEET Institute, thank you for allowing us to accompany you on this journey. We hope you continue to grow, continue to heal, and continue to deepen your relationship with yourself. May your nights become more restful, your days more meaningful, and your life more aligned with what matters most.

And whenever you find yourself struggling, remember this: The goal is not to force sleep; rather, the goal is to create a life, a mind, and a nervous system that no longer need to remain awake.

With gratitude,

Mardoche Sidor, MD
Karen Dubin, Ph.D., LCSW
The SWEET Institute
SWEET Institute Publishing
Transformational Books for a Transformational World

Acknowledgments

No book is ever written by one person alone. Every book is the product of countless conversations, experiences, teachers, mentors, colleagues, friends, family members, patients, students, and readers who contribute, directly or indirectly, to its creation. This book is no exception.

First and foremost, we would like to express our deepest gratitude to the thousands of individuals we have had the privilege of serving, teaching, coaching, supervising, and learning from over the years. As clinicians, educators, and students of human behavior, we have come to appreciate a simple truth: some of our greatest teachers are the very people who seek our help.

To the countless individuals who have shared their struggles with sleep, anxiety, trauma, grief, burnout, stress, perfectionism, and emotional suffering, thank you. Your courage, honesty, resilience, and willingness to share your stories have shaped our understanding of healing in ways no textbook ever could. Much of what appears in these pages was inspired by the lived experiences of people who entrusted us with their journeys.

We extend our heartfelt gratitude to the entire SWEET Institute community. Over the years, thousands of clinicians, social workers, psychologists, counselors, nurses, physicians, coaches, students, and helping professionals have participated in our courses, workshops, consultations, conferences, and learning communities. Their questions, insights, challenges, and reflections have continuously sharpened our thinking and deepened our understanding of what it truly takes to create lasting transformation.

To our presenters, collaborators, and contributors, thank you for your commitment to advancing the fields of mental health, personal growth, and human development. Your passion for learning and teaching continues to inspire us.

To our colleagues across psychiatry, psychology, social work, neuroscience, sleep medicine, behavioral medicine, public health, and the broader helping professions, we stand on the shoulders of your work. The scientific discoveries, clinical innovations, and theoretical frameworks developed by generations of researchers and practitioners have made this book possible.

We would also like to acknowledge the pioneers whose work influenced many of the ideas found throughout these pages. While too numerous to name individually, we are deeply indebted to the contributions of those who advanced our understanding of sleep science, attachment theory, trauma, psychodynamic psychology, cognitive behavioral therapy, mindfulness, neuroscience, existential psychology, humanistic psychology, and nervous system regulation.

A special thank-you goes to the readers of SWEET Institute Publishing. Every message, review, email, comment, question, and story reminds us why this work matters. Your support allows us to continue creating educational resources designed to bridge the gap between information and implementation, knowledge and action, understanding and transformation.

Mardoche would like to express personal gratitude to the many mentors, teachers, supervisors, colleagues, patients, and students who have influenced his professional and personal development over the years. He remains profoundly grateful for the opportunity to spend his life learning about the human mind, the human spirit, and the remarkable capacity people possess to heal, grow, and transform.

Karen would like to express her deepest gratitude to the clinicians, educators, leaders, helping professionals, and, most importantly, to the countless individuals, families, patients, students, and supervisees she has had the privilege of serving throughout her career. She remains profoundly grateful for the trust they have placed in her, for the lessons they have taught her, and for continually reminding her of the extraordinary resilience, strength, and capacity for growth that exists within every human being.

Finally, we wish to thank you, the reader. Of all the resources available to you, you chose to spend some of your time with this book. That is a gift we do not take lightly.

Whether you are reading these words because you struggle with sleep, care for someone who does, work in the helping professions, or simply wish to understand yourself more deeply, we are honored to accompany you on this journey.

We hope this book serves not only as a guide to better sleep, but also as a reminder that healing remains possible.

May you continue to learn. May you continue to grow. May you continue to heal. And may you find the deep rest that allows you to live fully awake.

With gratitude,

Mardoche Sidor, MD
Karen Dubin, Ph.D., LCSW
The SWEET Institute
SWEET Institute Publishing
Transformational Books for a Transformational World

Reader Integration Toolkit

Turning Insight Into Deep Sleep

One of the greatest challenges in personal growth, mental health, and behavior change is not learning new information. It is implementation.

Most people already know that sleep is important. Many already know they should reduce screen time, improve sleep hygiene, manage stress, exercise regularly, and create healthier routines. The challenge is rarely knowledge. The challenge is integration.

At the SWEET Institute, we believe transformation occurs when understanding moves through four stages:

Information → Awareness → Implementation → Integration

Information alone rarely changes lives. Practice does.

This toolkit is designed to help you bridge the gap between what you learned in this book and how you live moving forward.

Part I

The Deep Sleep Self-Assessment

Rate each item from 1–10.

- 1 = Strongly Disagree
- 10 = Strongly Agree

Biological Domain

___ I maintain a consistent wake-up time.

___ I receive adequate morning sunlight exposure.

___ I limit caffeine appropriately.

___ I engage in regular physical activity.

___ I have a bedtime routine.

___ My sleep environment supports restful sleep.

Psychological Domain

___ My internal dialogue is generally supportive.

___ I can tolerate uncertainty without becoming overwhelmed.

___ I manage stress effectively.

___ I can slow down without becoming highly anxious.

___ I am able to recognize when my thoughts are escalating fear.

Relational Domain

___ I have people I can talk to openly.

___ I feel emotionally supported.

___ My closest relationships contribute more to regulation than stress.

___ I feel connected to others.

Environmental Domain

___ My bedroom supports sleep.

___ Technology is not dominating my evenings.

___ My daily schedule allows time for restoration.

___ My environment feels reasonably safe and predictable.

Existential Domain

___ My life feels meaningful.

___ I have a sense of purpose.

___ I make time for activities that nourish my spirit.

___ My daily life aligns with my values.

Reflection

- Which domain received your lowest score?
- What is one action you can take to improve that domain?

Part II

The Four Layers of Transformation Worksheet

Layer 1: Conscious

- What behaviors currently interfere with your sleep?

____

____

____

____

____

____

- What new behaviors are you willing to begin?

____

____

____

____

____

____

Layer 2: Pre-Conscious

- What beliefs may be contributing to your sleep difficulties?

Examples:

- I must always stay alert.
- Rest is unproductive.
- I cannot relax.
- I have too much to do.

My beliefs:

____

____

____

____

____

____

Layer 3: Unconscious

- What emotions, experiences, or unresolved issues might your nervous system still be carrying?

____

____

____

____

____

____

Layer 4: Existential

- What would a well-rested life allow you to do, experience, or become?

____

____

____

____

____

____

Part III

The SWEET Body–Mind–Meaning Inventory

Body

- What does my body need more of?

____

____

____

____

____

____

- What does my body need less of?

____

____

____

____

____

____

Mind

- What thoughts consistently activate my nervous system?

- What thoughts support regulation?

Meaning

- What gives my life energy, purpose, and direction?

- What drains meaning from my life?

Part IV

The Deep Sleep Blueprint

Choose one commitment from each category.

Physical

- ☐ Consistent wake-up time
- ☐ Morning sunlight
- ☐ Daily movement
- ☐ Reduce caffeine
- ☐ Reduce alcohol

My commitment:

____

____

____

____

____

____

Psychological

- ☐ Daily mindfulness
- ☐ Breath awareness
- ☐ Journaling
- ☐ Gratitude practice
- ☐ Reduce self-criticism

My commitment:

____

____

____

____

____

____

Relational

- □ Reach out to one trusted person
- □ Ask for support
- □ Spend more time with nourishing relationships
- □ Strengthen boundaries

My commitment:

____

____

____

____

____

____

Existential

- ☐ Spend time in nature
- ☐ Engage in spiritual practice
- ☐ Volunteer
- ☐ Create
- ☐ Reflect on purpose

My commitment:

____

____

____

____

____

____

Part V

The 30-Day Deep Sleep Commitment

For the next 30 days, I commit to:

____

____

____

____

____

____

Why is this commitment important to me?

____

____

____

____

____

____

What will improve in my life if I follow through?

____

____

____

____

____

____

Signature: ____________________

Date: ________________________

Part VI

The Nightly Reflection

Before bed, spend two minutes answering:

- What am I carrying tonight?

____

____

____

____

____

____

- What can I release until tomorrow?

____

____

____

____

____

____

- What does my nervous system need right now?

- What am I grateful for?

- One compassionate statement to myself:

Final Reflection

Imagine that six months have passed. You are sleeping well. You wake up feeling restored. Your nervous system feels calmer. Your life feels more aligned.

Write a letter from that future version of yourself to the person you are today. What would they want you to know?

Future Self Letter

Reflection Prompt

Imagine it is 6–12 months from now.

You are sleeping deeply.

You wake feeling restored.

Your nervous system feels calmer.

Your life feels more aligned.

Write a letter from your future self to the present you.

Letter

Dear Present Me,

I know how exhausted you have been.
I know how hard things have felt.
What I want you to know is that things did change.

Here is what helped most:

What I wish you had stopped worrying about:

What became possible once sleep improved:

What I want you to keep remembering:

With gratitude,
Your Future Self

Nightly Reflection Card

Before sleep, pause and ask:

1. What am I carrying tonight?

2. What can I release until tomorrow?

3. What does my body need right now?

4. What am I grateful for?

5. One compassionate statement to myself:

Closing Breath

Inhale: I am here.

Exhale: I can let go.

Repeat five times.

Remember

You do not have to implement everything. You only have to begin: one habit, one insight, one practice, one breath, one evening, and one night at a time.

Transformation is not created by intensity. It is created by consistency; and what is repeated becomes strengthened.

May you strengthen rest, your peace, your awareness, your relationship with yourself; and may you sleep deeply.

Mardoche Sidor, MD
Karen Dubin, Ph.D., LCSW
The SWEET Institute

Appendix

Tools, Exercises, Charts, and Frameworks

How to Use This Appendix

Throughout Deep Sleep, we have emphasized a central principle:

Transformation occurs through implementation.

The purpose of this appendix is to help you move from understanding to action, from information to experience, and from insight to sustainable change.

You do not need to complete every exercise, or use every tool. Instead, choose the tools that resonate most strongly with you and apply them consistently.

Remember:

Small actions, repeated consistently, create profound transformation.

SECTION 1

The SWEET Model of Deep Sleep

An Integrated Framework for Restorative Sleep

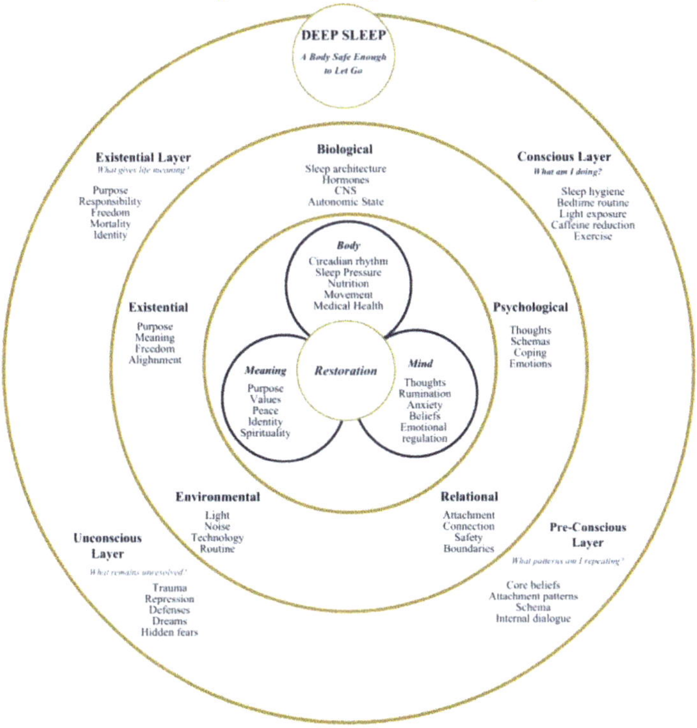

SWEET Sleep Formula

Stabilize → Decide → Act → Feel → Repeat

The SWEET Four Layers of Transformation Framework

Every sleep challenge can be explored through four interconnected layers.

Layer	Question	Focus
Conscious	What am I doing?	Habits, routines, behavior
Pre-Conscious	What patterns am I repeating?	Beliefs, schemas, attachment
Unconscious	What remains unresolved?	Repressed emotions, defenses, dreams
Existential	What gives life meaning?	Purpose, values, freedom, identity

Reflection Exercise

Which layer currently deserves the most attention?

□ Conscious

□ Pre-Conscious

□ Unconscious

□ Existential

Why?

SECTION 2

The SWEET Multi-Domain Sleep Assessment

Every sleep difficulty exists simultaneously across five domains.

Domain	Key Question
Biological	What is happening in my body?
Psychological	What is happening in my mind?
Relational	How are relationships affecting me?
Environmental	What environmental factors matter?
Existential	What role does meaning play?

Exercise

Rate each domain from 1–10.

Biological _________

Psychological _________

Relational _________

Environmental _________

Existential _________

Lowest score: _________

One action step:

SECTION 3

The SWEET Body–Mind–Meaning Framework

Body

What does my body need?

- □ Sleep
- □ Exercise
- □ Nutrition
- □ Hydration
- □ Relaxation
- □ Medical evaluation

Mind

What does my mind need?

- □ Calm
- □ Flexibility
- □ Perspective
- □ Emotional processing
- □ Reduced self-criticism

Meaning

What does my life need?

- □ Purpose
- □ Connection
- □ Joy
- □ Creativity
- □ Spirituality
- □ Service

Reflection:

Which dimension needs the most attention?

____

____

____

____

____

____

SECTION 4

The SWEET SDAF Framework

Stabilize → Decide → Act → Feel

Before making important decisions:

Step 1: Stabilize

Ask:

What state is my nervous system currently in?

- □ Calm
- □ Activated
- □ Overwhelmed
- □ Exhausted

Step 2: Decide

What would my wisest self-choose?

____

____

____

____

____

____

Step 3: Act

What is the next step?

Step 4: Feel

What happened?

SECTION 5

Sleep Hygiene Checklist

Morning

□ Wake at consistent time

□ Morning sunlight exposure

□ Hydration

□ Movement

Afternoon

□ Limit caffeine after noon

□ Manage stress proactively

□ Physical activity

Evening

□ Dim lights

□ Reduce stimulation

□ Reduce screen exposure

□ Light meal

□ Wind-down ritual

Bedroom

- □ Cool temperature
- □ Dark environment
- □ Quiet environment
- □ Comfortable bedding

SECTION 6

The Deep Sleep Blueprint

The 5 Foundations

Foundation 1: Rhythm

- Consistent wake-up time

Foundation 2: Regulation

- Daily nervous system practices

Foundation 3: Reflection

- Awareness of thoughts and emotions

Foundation 4: Relationship

- Supportive connection

Foundation 5: Meaning

- Purpose and alignment

Current strongest foundation:

____

____

____

____

____

Current weakest foundation:

SECTION 7

Internal Dialogue Audit

Write three common nighttime thoughts.

1.

2.

3.

Now challenge each thought.

What is another possible perspective?

SECTION 8

Dream Reflection Worksheet

Dream Summary:

____

____

____

____

____

____

Emotions Present:

- □ Fear
- □ Sadness
- □ Anger
- □ Joy
- □ Shame
- □ Confusion
- □ Longing

Possible Symbolism:

Connection to Current Life:

SECTION 9

Nervous System Regulation Menu

Choose three daily practices.

Physical

- □ Walking
- □ Stretching
- □ Exercise
- □ Hydration
- □ Breath awareness

Psychological

- □ Journaling
- □ Meditation
- □ Reading
- □ Gratitude
- □ Therapy

Relational

- □ Conversation
- □ Community
- □ Family time
- □ Peer support

Existential

- □ Prayer
- □ Nature
- □ Creativity
- □ Service
- □ Reflection

My Three Daily Practices:

1.

____

____

____

____

____

____

2.

____

____

____

____

____

____

3.

SECTION 10

The Deep Sleep Trigger Tracker

Date: ___________

Sleep Quality (1–10): _______

Triggers Today:

- □ Stress
- □ Conflict
- □ Caffeine
- □ Alcohol
- □ Technology
- □ Work
- □ Loneliness
- □ Health concerns
- □ Other

Notes:

SECTION 11

The 30-Day Deep Sleep Challenge

Daily Checklist

- □ Morning sunlight
- □ Consistent wake-up time
- □ Physical movement
- □ Reduced caffeine
- □ Breath awareness
- □ Reflection practice
- □ Reduced evening technology
- □ Gratitude
- □ Bedtime ritual

Weekly Review

What worked?

____

____

____

____

____

____

What did not work?

What will I continue?

Recommended Reading

Sleep Science

- *Why We Sleep*

  Matthew Walker, PhD

  The modern classic on sleep science. A comprehensive overview of sleep architecture, circadian rhythms, dreaming, memory consolidation, health outcomes, and the societal impact of sleep deprivation.
- *The Promise of Sleep*

  William C. Dement, MD, PhD

  Written by one of the founders of sleep medicine, this book provides foundational knowledge about sleep disorders and the importance of restorative sleep.
- *Say Good Night to Insomnia*
- Gregg D. Jacobs, PhD
- One of the earliest accessible introductions to cognitive behavioral approaches for insomnia.

Nervous System Regulation and Trauma

- *The Body Keeps the Score*

  Bessel van der Kolk, MD

  A landmark work exploring how trauma affects the brain, body, nervous system, and long-term health.
- *In an Unspoken Voice: How the body releases trauma and restores goodness*

  Peter A. Levine, PhD

  An important exploration of trauma, embodiment, and nervous system healing.

- *The Polyvagal Theory*

  Stephen W. Porges, PhD

  Foundational reading for understanding safety, connection, autonomic regulation, and the nervous system.

Mindfulness and Emotional Regulation

- *Full Catastrophe Living*

  Jon Kabat-Zinn, PhD

  A practical and evidence-based guide to mindfulness, stress reduction, and emotional well-being.
- *Wherever You Go, There You Are*

  Jon Kabat-Zinn, PhD

  A concise and accessible introduction to mindfulness practice.

—

Psychology and Human Development

- *The Developing Mind*

  Daniel J. Siegel, MD

  A groundbreaking integration of neuroscience, attachment, emotional development, and interpersonal neurobiology.
- *Attached*

  Amir Levine, MD, and Rachel Heller, MA

  A highly practical introduction to attachment theory and adult relationships.
- *Reinventing Your Life*

  Jeffrey Young, PhD, and Janet Klosko, PhD

  One of the most accessible introductions to schema therapy and long-standing emotional patterns.

Acceptance, Flexibility, and Psychological Resilience

- *Get Out of Your Mind and Into Your Life*

  Steven C. Hayes, PhD

  A practical introduction to Acceptance and Commitment Therapy (ACT).
- *A Liberated Mind*

  Steven C. Hayes, PhD

  An exploration of psychological flexibility and sustainable well-being.

—

Meaning, Purpose, and the Existential Layer

- *Man's Search for Meaning*

  Viktor E. Frankl, MD

  One of the most influential books ever written on meaning, resilience, suffering, and human freedom.
- *Existential Psychotherapy*

  Irvin D. Yalom, MD

  A classic exploration of meaning, mortality, freedom, responsibility, and authentic living.

More from SWEET Institute Publishing

Transformational Books for a Transformational World

At SWEET Institute Publishing, we believe lasting change occurs when individuals move beyond information and into implementation, transformation, and integration. The following titles expand upon many of the themes explored in Deep Sleep and provide practical frameworks for healing, growth, leadership, self-awareness, and meaningful living. SWEET Institute Publishing focuses on mental health, wellness, clinical practice, leadership, habits, identity, and personal transformation.

For Readers Interested in Nervous System Healing and Emotional Wellness

- *Always Enough: The Transformational Power of Unconditional Positive Regard*
- *Before Anything Else, Validate: The Missing Link in Healing, Leadership, Relationships, and Personal Growth*
- *Discovering Your Worth: Everything You Need to Feel Fulfilled*
- *Emotional Intelligence: The Inner Science of Transformation*
- *Journey to Empowerment*
- *Life Is Not Hard: A New Blueprint for Living with Ease, Meaning, and Freedom*
- *The Anxiety Course: The Workbook*
- *Worthy: From Self-Doubt to Self-Respect*

For Readers Interested in Habits, Identity, and Sustainable Change

- *One Habit at a Time: The Art and Science of Sustainable Change*
- *Remembering: The Journey Back to the Pre-Conditioned Self*
- *The Secret Is in Remembering: Why We Suffer, Why We Forget, and How to Return to Who We Are*
- *It's All Perfect: What If Nothing in Your Life Was a Mistake?*
- *Becoming the Very Best*

For Clinicians, Coaches, and Helping Professionals

- *The Clinician's Mirror: A Story of Projection, Self-Awareness, and Transformation for Clinicians*
- *NLP for Clinicians*
- *The Psychotherapy Certificate Course: The Clinician and Coach Manual (Books 1–3)*
- *The Courage to Care: Stories of Healing, Hope, and the Power of Social Work*
- *The Psychiatric Nurse Practitioner's Handbook: Healing with Precision, Presence, and Power*

For Leaders, Organizations, and Systems Change

- *Because of Us: Why Outcomes Change When We Do*
- *Transforming Team Relationships from the Inside Out: The SWEET Healing Circle for Agencies*
- *Designing Care That Works: A Step-by-Step Guide to Building Programs that Heal*

- *Beyond Burnout: The Inside-Out Revolution in Work, Healing, and Meaning*
- *Playing* Small: How We Shrink Ourselves, How We Rise, and Who We Become

For Readers Exploring Meaning, Faith, and Consciousness

- *Determined to See: A Science-Based and Story-Driven Integration of A Course in Miracles and the Four Layers of Transformation*
- *The Power of Faith: A Harvard-Trained Psychiatrist Speaking on Faith*
- *The Power of Belief: How Ideas Shape Leaders, Nations, and the Future*
- *The Joy We* Bring: Rediscovering the Power of Joy in Everyday Life

Special Titles

- *Unshakable Women: Reclaiming Power, Purpose, and Presence in Leadership*
- *Never Give Up: A Memoir of Resilience, Purpose, and Becoming the Change — by Gary Jenkins*, D.A., MPA

Continue the Journey

If Deep Sleep helped you better understand your nervous system, restore your relationship with rest, and reconnect with yourself, we invite you to continue the journey through the growing collection of books, courses, communities, and resources offered by the SWEET Institute Publishing. SWEET Institute was created to bridge the gap between science and practice, knowledge and implementation, healing and transformation.

About the Authors

Mardoche Sidor, MD

Mardoche Sidor, MD, is a Harvard-trained psychiatrist, educator, speaker, and founder of the SWEET Institute. He is quadruple board-certified in Adult Psychiatry, Child and Adolescent Psychiatry, Addiction Psychiatry, and Forensic Psychiatry, with additional training in Community Psychiatry and Geriatric Psychiatry. Throughout his career, he has worked across a wide range of clinical, academic, leadership, and community settings, dedicating his life to understanding human behavior, psychological healing, and personal transformation.

Dr. Sidor has spent years teaching mental health professionals, developing innovative educational programs, and helping individuals bridge the gap between insight and action. His work integrates neuroscience, psychotherapy, mindfulness, psychodynamic understanding, behavioral science, existential psychology, and practical strategies for sustainable change. He is particularly passionate about helping people understand that many of the challenges they face are not signs of weakness, but opportunities for growth, healing, and self-discovery.

As an educator, Dr. Sidor has taught thousands of clinicians through seminars, certificate programs, conferences, consultation groups, and professional development initiatives. As a psychiatrist, he remains deeply committed to understanding the whole person: body, mind, relationships, environment, and meaning, and helping individuals move from survival to flourishing.

His writing reflects the same philosophy that guides his clinical and educational work: meaningful transformation occurs when knowledge becomes experience, experience becomes action, and action becomes integrated into daily life.

Karen Dubin, PhD., LCSW

Karen Dubin, PhD., LCSW, is a social worker, educator, author, and co-founder of the SWEET Institute. For more than two decades, she has dedicated her career to helping individuals, clinicians, and organizations cultivate greater self-awareness, emotional resilience, and meaningful, lasting change. Her work integrates evidence-based clinical practice with a deep respect for the complexity of the human experience and an enduring belief in people's capacity to heal, grow, and thrive.

Dr. Dubin is widely recognized for her ability to translate complex psychological and neuroscientific concepts into practical, accessible strategies that people can apply in their professional and personal lives. Throughout her career, she has trained thousands of helping professionals, mentored clinicians, and created learning experiences that bridge research with real-world practice.

Her approach is grounded in compassion, curiosity, personal responsibility, and the belief that meaningful change begins with greater awareness. Whether teaching, supervising, or providing clinical care, she encourages individuals to move beyond self-limiting patterns, strengthen their relationships, and live with greater authenticity, purpose, and psychological flexibility.

Dr. Dubin remains deeply committed to advancing the helping professions by fostering learning communities that encourage critical thinking, meaningful connection, and lifelong professional and personal growth.

The SWEET Institute

The SWEET Institute is an educational organization dedicated to transforming mental health and social services through education, community, and innovation. Founded on the belief that learning should be practical, experiential, and transformative, the Institute provides continuing education, professional development, certificate programs, consultation, coaching, and community-based learning opportunities for clinicians and helping professionals throughout the world.

At the heart of the Institute's work is a simple but powerful belief: information alone rarely changes lives. Transformation occurs when knowledge is translated into awareness, action, consistency, and integration.

The SWEET Institute's educational philosophy is reflected in its Four Layers of Transformation framework, which explores change at the conscious, pre-conscious, unconscious, and existential levels. This model, along with the SWEET Multi-Domain Model, the Body–Mind–Meaning Framework, and the SDAF Framework, forms the foundation of many of the Institute's programs, publications, and educational offerings.

Through books, courses, conferences, communities, and collaborative learning experiences, the SWEET Institute seeks to empower individuals and professionals to grow, heal, lead, and create meaningful change in their lives and the lives of others.

To learn more about the SWEET Institute and its educational offerings, visit the official website of SWEET Institute.

SWEET Institute Publishing
Transformational Books for a Transformational World

www.ingramcontent.com/pod-product-compliance
Lightning Source LLC
LaVergne TN
LVHW050908210926
848482LV00012B/373